LAUNCHERS

LAUNCHERS

DON'T JUST TAKE A JOB, LAUNCH YOUR CAREER!

DR. KERRY LITZENBERG AND CODIE WRIGHT

geekdom media

COPYRIGHT © 2019 KERRY K. LITZENBERG & CODIE J. WRIGHT

LAUNCHERS

Don't Just Take a Job, Launch Your Career!

ISBN   978-1-5445-1356-0 *Paperback*

978-1-5445-1355-3 *Ebook*

Dr. Kerry Litzenberg: I dedicate this book to my wife, Sandy, my three daughters, Karen, Jane, and Sara, and to my fabulous sons-in-law, Jimmy and Matt, as well as the truly outstanding grandchildren they have produced, Riley, Trey, Kennedy, Reed, and Reece. These people have been a true blessing in my life.

Codie Wright: I dedicate this book to my mom for teaching me the importance of a strong work ethic, and to my father, who taught me how to have the biggest heart.

Together, we would like to dedicate this book, as well as our careers, to the many young people we've had the privilege of helping launch their professional careers.

Finally, we dedicate our lives to our Lord and Savior, Jesus Christ.

CONTENTS

INTRODUCTION

HOW TO USE THIS BOOK, *WHY* WE
WROTE IT, AND *WHO* IT'S FOR

You are about to make the most exciting decision of your entire life: to launch your career.

Meet Sam, a twenty-two-year-old who majored in business at a top-tier university. Over the course of four years, Sam took a wide variety of marketing, management, and business classes geared toward a degree plan for his major. He was involved in several organizations and volunteer activities, earned a 3.2 GPA, and had a part-time job during school to earn a little extra income.

When he first entered college, Sam's goal was to earn a degree in biomedical science and then attend medical school. After countless hours of study and poor test scores, he realized that chemistry and biology were not a good fit, so he decided to switch to a business degree. "A business degree will provide a wide range of opportunities," he thought, "so why don't I check out that option?"

Sam was an excellent candidate for a marketing or management position, but there was one problem: he didn't know which industry or company was the *best fit* for his career. While meandering through the university's business career fair one day, he stumbled upon a software company that seemed somewhat interesting, so he applied and was offered a position.

Sam took the job and worked for the company for several years, but decided it wasn't a good cultural fit for him. He left for a "better" job in a different industry, where he stayed for several more years, before he decided it wasn't better after all. This same vicious cycle continued for the next five years, until Sam eventually accepted a position in the medical industry. Will it finally be a good fit for him? Time will tell.

Does this cycle sound familiar? Does it remind you of anyone you know?

If this situation stresses you out, you're not alone. Many people between the ages of twenty-one and thirty-five are feeling anxious about the process of preparing for their career launch. You may be one of them. Maybe you feel like you don't have enough time to prepare. Maybe no one has ever shared with you the process for launching yourself into the next three or four *decades* of your life.

Let us put your mind at ease. There's no reason to worry. With the right plan in place, a clear sense of what you have to offer, and an understanding of the context of your career space, you can launch yourself into your career with clarity and purpose. However, it's a major effort, so we encourage you to start your launch now. The last thing we want is for you to just take a job and wind up feeling miserable. Become a Launcher—that's what we call people who have begun this process—and start preparing for a satisfying and fulfilling career now.

We work primarily with college students, and we're always amazed to meet people who will work for four or five years in college learning about supporting subjects for their major, but then spend *no time* preparing for the actual career launch. In fact, many college students wait until they graduate and then simply start looking for a job with no plan in place. There seems to be an assumption that somehow the pieces will fall into place on their own, but it doesn't work that way. If you don't create a calculated career launch, you will end up job hunting and most likely take the first job that comes along. You might have four to five jobs in the next five years that you don't like while you wait for the right one.

Think of your career launch like the space program. When NASA wants to launch the latest communications satellite into space, they discuss, test, and develop a plan for months, possibly years, before they finally push the launch button on the rocket that will take the satellite into space.

The launch itself lasts a matter of minutes, and getting the satellite into orbit might take two hours. It all happens so quickly that it can seem sudden to outside observers who don't necessarily see the careful thought and planning that went into making sure the launch was a success, but it was the planning that made it possible. Remember, even though the launch happened quickly, that satellite is going to orbit the earth for many years, which is why all of the planning and preparation are well worth it.

That's what a career launch is like under the best of circumstances. Plan, plan, plan, then push the launch button and hope for a successful launch.

A CHANGING FOCUS

In high school and the early college years, maybe you were like most students—focused on your studies and extracurricular activities. You worried about grades, your SAT, LSAT, GRE, or GMAT scores, and you just hoped your career would unfold naturally along the way.

Friends and family have asked you from a young age, "What are you going to be when you grow up?" That's an easy question to ask, but maybe no one has ever shown you how to realize your best answer to that question.

When you applied to college, your immediate concern was selecting a major. However, we tend to find that students select a major based on how well they performed in a certain subject or extracurricular activity during high school. "I aced my English classes," they might think, "so maybe I should major in English." Sometimes, they choose a major based on a general interest in a subject: "I love animals, so maybe I'll be a veterinarian."

However, the selection of a college major might not match well with a long-term career plan. In fact, some of the majors that are frequently chosen don't readily lend themselves to career options. Psychology is a common undergraduate major, but unless a student continues their education into the graduate level, a psychology degree won't open up many doors other than clinical psychology.

In our experience, many college professors know very little about the relevance of their curriculum in finding a career. That's not really their job anyway, but this is where many students falter. They spend a hundred thousand dollars learning English or chemistry or some other subject; by the end, they've learned almost nothing about how to use that knowledge and the skills they've gained to launch a career in a relevant industry that matters to them.

We're not faulting the university system. A degree program promises to teach students particular subjects, and that's what it does. When students come to the end of their degree program, they might be handed over to a career center, but career centers often have very few contacts or experience in specific industry career paths. If you go there as an English major, they will help you with your résumé but, more than likely, they won't have industry connections to help you find a specific job opportunity.

Many graduates reach this point and are shocked to find out how ill-prepared they are to find an industry and company culture that suits them. The disconnect between academia and industry is substantial. To a college freshman, four years seems like a really long time, but in reality those four years go by very quickly. We suggest students identify the industries that interest them and start making plans by the beginning of their senior year, but we meet many students who are in their very last semester of college and still have absolutely no idea what they want to do with their lives.

If you are at that point now, or even if you're already out of college, don't worry. We're here to help with your career launch.

FEAR OF FAILURE

Parents and other loved ones might start pestering you as you approach graduation. "What are you going to do for a living? Where are you going to work?" If you haven't put a lot of thought into it, these questions can make you start to feel *very* overwhelmed.

Adding to the problem, your parents and other adults in your life have been telling you since you were a child that you can be anything you want to be when you grow up. From their perspective, since they have provided vague encouragement and motivation, they feel as if you should already know what you want to do; in reality, this can intensify your fear of failure.

In order to allay the fear and get your parents off your back, you might be tempted to just *take a job*. If you haven't planned and chosen the right *career*, the job won't resonate with you. It will just be mindless work. After a few months or a year, you will find yourself struggling with anxiety and depression, feeling stuck and wishing you were back in college—the *good old days*. Whenever we hear people tell college students, "Stay in school, the real world is hard," we know that's a person who probably didn't launch their career well and didn't enjoy the position they selected.

Unfortunately, it's much harder to get another job once you're working fifty hours a week. You no longer have as much time for research or interviews, so the job can feel like a *dead-end street*. We believe this is a major cause of the current widespread dissatisfaction that twenty-one to thirty-five-year-olds feel at work.

Here's the good news: whether you're approaching graduation or already struggling with an unsatisfying job postgraduation, you can get on the right path. You don't have to take the first thing that comes along, and you don't have to keep slogging away in an unsatisfying job.

You get to determine what you want out of your career, so why waste the next thirty years at a job that you dread or despise? When you pursue your passion, you will increase your own sense of engagement and fulfillment.

PUT YOUR CAREER LAUNCH INTO ACTION
In this book, we present a plan for successfully *launch-*

ing or *relaunching* your career. We know your future is important to you, so we're going to help you plan for the next thirty or forty years by getting off on the right foot. We want to come along with you on the journey. You don't have to do this all by yourself.

However, the plan isn't instantaneous. You can't press the launch button and suddenly have an amazing career, and it won't happen over a weekend. However, it might not be as time-consuming as you imagine. In the following chapters, you will begin to gain a clear sense of what you bring to the table—your skills and personality and the knowledge you've acquired in college—and learn how all of those things fit together to provide the fuel for your launch. We'll help you determine your launch criteria so you can identify and select an industry and company that resonate with you. Finally, we will help you understand the culture of your ideal workplace so you can make the transition successfully.

OUR STORY AND OUR VISION

Now, you might ask yourself, "Who are you, and why should I listen to you?" That's a great question, so let us introduce ourselves. We are Codie Wright and Dr. Kerry Litzenberg, and we help students and young adults prepare for and implement their career launches through the Weston AgriFood Sales Program at Texas A&M University.

Dr. Litzenberg has forty years of university experience helping Launchers just like you to make the transition from graduation to full-time employment. To fulfill that vision, he has done much research on how students can use the knowledge they acquire in college to enjoy a successful career.

To help students identify the skills they have to offer for their career launch, he published the Agribusiness Management and Aptitude Skills Survey (AgriMASS) in 1987. However, it was the book *Emotional Intelligence*, written by psychologist Daniel Goleman in 1995, that finally explained something Dr. Litzenberg had been trying to articulate for twenty years. What became clear through Goleman's theory was that, rather than simply figuring out their skills, students must come to *know themselves* first.

Emotional intelligence is the human side of your career launch—the ability to understand your emotions (self-awareness) and how you act or react to emotional triggers (self-management). That's why, when we help Launchers like you with your career launch, we first teach you to know yourself. Only then do we help you find your desired industry and company culture and determine if you are a good fit.

Codie Wright, as a student in Dr. Litzenberg's sales class

in 2013, saw firsthand how many of her peers became overwhelmed with the prospect of getting a job. She shared their anxiety as they approached graduation with little preparation or planning about their impending career launches. She also saw friends struggling postgraduation, simply taking jobs instead of successfully launching careers and dealing with the ensuing unhappiness.

She decided she wanted to be part of the solution, so while earning her master's degree, she reached out to Dr. Litzenberg. "I'm passionate about sales," she said. "I love the industry, and your class really resonated with me. How can we work together to help students?" As it turned out, he had an open position, and that's how our professional partnership began.

Working together, we now help students understand the career launch space so they can make the transition from university to their professional lives. Our advice isn't limited to college students, however. We've met many young people between the ages of twenty-one and thirty-five who can benefit from proper career planning and preparation. Some are launching into their first career, and others are relaunching after an unsuccessful transition.

A NOTE TO PARENTS

In working with Launchers, we have come to realize the important role parents play. If you happen to be a parent reading this book because you're looking to help your son or daughter launch their career, we understand your frustration. We've heard parents say, "We spent a hundred thousand dollars on our child's education, and what have they done with it? When are they going to get a job?"

You deserve credit for raising a great kid. You've done so much for them over the years, taking them to soccer, ballet, dance, checking on their grades, talking to their teachers and making sure they took the right classes. You deserve thanks for that, but it's so important to want more for your child than to simply get them out of the house and start earning some kind of living. Being able to post, "My kid got a job," on Facebook is nice, but if your child winds up in the wrong career—in a job that is a poor fit for their skills, experience, and personality—you're helping to set them up for an unpleasant and possibly failed career launch.

We strongly encourage you not to think in terms of a job. Getting a job might feel good in the short term, but it doesn't contribute to long-term success. Your child's drive will become relentless when paired with passion, and determining what interests them will increase their overall quality of life. Ultimately, don't you want your children to be happy and fulfilled? If you want to contribute to their success, the most important thing you can do is to help them focus on launching their career in the right industry and the right company culture.

DELIVERABLES TO SELF

This book isn't meant to be simply a self-help book full of encouragement and positivity. Rather, it provides a *clear-cut set of directions*, creating a useful guide for launching or relaunching a career. Think of it as a handbook for the journey.

While the information provided in the coming chapters can be useful for older people looking to change careers, our advice is geared primarily for twenty-one to thirty-five-year-olds. To that end, we will discuss ways to navigate the differing generational expectations that are inevitable in a professional environment.

Many of the chapters include "Deliverables to Self" because we believe you must give our concepts time to percolate in your thinking. It's too easy to get so busy living life that you forget to think about *how* you want to live life.

These deliverables are practical activities for which you are responsible to yourself. Complete them over the next few months, and you will be on your way to a great career launch.

We also intend to give you the resources you need all the way through your career selection process and even as you integrate into the workplace. Before we get there, however, we will begin by answering the most important question:

"How do I get started?"

RECOMMENDED READING

Along with the book you're holding in your hands right now, we think there are many other books that can help you on the journey toward your career launch. Therefore, in a few places throughout the book, we will provide further recommendations, beginning with the following:

Do What You Are: Discover the Perfect Career for You Through the Secrets of Personality Type by Paul D. Tieger, Barbara Barron, and Kelly Tieger

Outliers: The Story of Success by Malcolm Gladwell

PART ONE

CREATING YOUR CAREER LAUNCH PLAN

1

EVERYONE KEEPS ASKING ME, "WHAT ARE YOU GOING TO BE?"

When Codie was an undergraduate, she worked at a quaint little store called Catalena Hatters that sells high-quality, custom-made felt and straw hats in downtown Bryan, Texas. With limited financial support from her parents, this was how she worked her way through college. She spent so much time in the store that it practically became her home away from home.

On a particular Saturday morning, she was sitting behind the counter and sipping coffee while the store owner, Scott Catalena, shaped a hat in the corner when a family entered the store. They had a cute little four-year-old boy with them, and he was thoroughly excited to see all the hats. Codie began interacting with him, and as she did, she casually asked a question that adults often ask children.

"What do you want to be when you grow up?"

The little boy turned to her, gave her a serious look, and said, "When I grow up, I'm going to be a ninja billionaire."

At the time, everyone laughed, and Codie thought, "Wow, this kid has a huge imagination," but later, reflecting on his answer, she had a realization. That little boy is almost certainly *not* going to be a ninja billionaire. "What am I doing asking him what he wants to be when he grows up?" she thought. "He's four years old. He has no idea what opportunities exist out there in the world."

When we ask children this question, their response is usually shaped by what they've been exposed to. That's why so many of them will say firefighter, doctor, or teacher. In the case of that little boy, he had probably been influenced by TV shows or YouTube videos or he had an extremely creative imagination. After all, there just aren't many real, live ninja billionaires in the world. In fact, if you *are* one or happen to come across one, please let us know.

That little boy will be asked that same question throughout his childhood and teenage years and right into college, but eventually, people will start to ask with mounting nervousness and concern.

PRESSURED BY SOCIETY

By the time you reach your undergraduate years, chances are you've been asked some form of the question hundreds of times. "What are you going to be when you grow up? What do you want to do with your life? What are you going to *become*?" Like many young adults, you might feel pressured by society. Everyone expects you to have an answer, no matter how young, uncertain, or unprepared you are.

The implication of these questions is that it's almost magical: "You can be anything you want to be, so what do you want to be? *Decide!*"

In reality, you *can't* be anything you want to be. We all have skills, experience, and personalities that make us more suited for some careers than for others. You have to take an inventory of *who* you are and what you've *done* so you can choose a career path that fits. Don't forget, there are millions and millions of young adults preparing to enter the workforce, so if you want to stand out, you have to differentiate yourself.

SNOW PLOW PARENTS

Your parents have supported you and helped you get to where you are today. Most of us appreciate having parents who are present, active, and engaged in our lives, but maybe you've heard the term "helicopter parents," which refers to parents who hover around their children throughout their lives. People who use this term generally mean it in a negative way. We prefer the term "snow plow parents" because that's what we often see. Like a snow plow, these parents spend their lives trying to clear every obstacle out of the way for their children to make the ride as smooth and easy as possible.

A parent of one of our students scheduled a meeting to speak with us about her son's future. We don't typically have these kinds of conversations with parents, and her opening question took us by surprise. Instead of a casual conversation about her son's progress and potential, she opened by asking, "What do I need to do to make sure my son has a job?"

Astonished, we replied, "You can't do much. Ask your son to meet with us, and we'll help him get started on his own career process."

This isn't unusual. We've heard stories of parents negotiating with companies to try to get their children what they thought was a better job offer. In one case, a father called a company and said, "I don't think your offer is good enough for my daughter. She needs more vacation time." As crazy as this sounds, in our experience, these kinds of negotiations have become commonplace for Launchers.

From the time you were little, your parents provided love and encouragement. They supported you and told you that you can be anything you want to be. They've even tried to clear the obstacles out of your path to make it as easy as possible. In doing so, they believed they were giving you autonomy, but in reality, it can produce *analysis paralysis* if you don't know what you want to do. If you've received years of encouragement but no clear process for finding the *right* career path, you might feel pressured to take the first job that comes along after graduation. This, in turn, has led to widespread dissatisfaction at work, which has contributed to a dramatic rise in employee turnover.

It's a toxic mix that costs a lot of money. Companies spend money to recruit someone right out of college, pay for drug testing, pay for their training, and eighteen months later, the new employee says, "I don't see my value here, I'm not sure what I'm contributing, and I don't enjoy this position," and they leave.

Some companies have attempted to compensate by hiring more people, knowing only a few will stick around. In fact, we've heard company leaders that we work with say, "We're going to hire ten people because in two years, only the five best will still be here." They plan for widespread loss from the beginning, creating an immediate toxicity from day one. This situation has gotten noticeably worse in the last eight to ten years.

We want Launchers to be absolutely positive when they accept a career position that it is where they will stay for a long time.

TAKING A JOB VERSUS LAUNCHING A CAREER

If you are told your entire life, "You can be anything you want to be," it creates a disconnect between what you *want* to be and what you *can* be. As a result, you might fail to make optimal use of your skills, personality, and education when choosing a career.

We had a psychology major approach us and say, "I want to sell agricultural chemicals for a living." It never occurred to him that the incompatibility of this desire with his major might be a hindrance. He hadn't studied any of the necessary skills, taken any relevant classes, or developed the right expertise to sell agricultural chemicals, but he never considered that this might be a problem.

Suppose you find yourself at a career fair, and you come

across several companies that are offering positions. As you evaluate the first one, you think, "I might be able to do this. I guess I could see myself working there." Are you specifically weighing your desires, skills, and knowledge, or are you simply crossing your fingers and hoping for the best?

Launching a career means having a clearly defined goal. It's about identifying your skills and determining what resonates with you in order to be successful in a specific industry. It's about bringing everything you have to the table, leveraging your network and mentors to move you forward in the process, and ultimately, becoming a thought leader in your chosen profession.

DON'T WASTE YOUR TWENTIES

We don't want you to get the idea that the deck is stacked against you or that most students are experiencing terrible career launches. On the contrary, we've seen many students go through a career-planning process while thinking carefully about their career launch, who wound up enjoying tremendous success in their chosen field.

We want this for every Launcher, including *you*.

However, we see too many students who jump from job to job and never land anywhere. At a freshman orientation, we heard one of the deans actually tell a student, "We know you're going to have four or five jobs by the time you're thirty. That's just what happens."

We approached the dean after orientation and said, "Please, don't encourage this kind of behavior. It sets up bleak expectations both for students and companies. We are working very hard to make sure what you said isn't true."

Working in a job you don't like for years while looking for a job you might love is a tremendous drain on your emotions. Not loving your job spills over into your life outside of work. Many people may not notice this type of workplace depression, but it is a significant factor in a lot of dissatisfaction with the overall quality of life.

As a Launcher, you have so much to offer the world, and you *will* have a great career launch if you focus on your strengths and interests. You don't have to find yourself in your late twenties or early thirties working at a job that is way below your skill level, feeling unhappy and stuck. Even if you've already experienced a bad career launch, it's not too late. You can begin to implement a plan for a successful relaunch.

We know of one young man who worked in the tech industry for three years, found himself incredibly unhappy, then switched to the pharmaceutical industry, where he is thriving. He's proof that a relaunch can work.

However, he essentially wasted those three years in tech. None of the knowledge or industry experience he'd acquired during those three years applied to his new role in the pharmaceutical industry. Fortunately, he found the right career with his relaunch, but why waste years in a job that doesn't make you happy and that you're not very good at? Doesn't it make more sense to get it right from the beginning? Ideally, you won't have to relaunch because you'll get it right the first time (though, if you do, it's not the end of the world).

Codie had a conversation once with a young woman who had graduated from a college in Virginia.

"What are you doing these days?" Codie asked.

"Oh, I've been bartending," the girl replied.

"Out of curiosity, what was your degree?"

"I have a bachelor's degree in business," the girl said. "I would love to get into pharmaceutical sales, but I just wanted to take a couple years off before I get into the groove. That's why I'm bartending."

"Have you considered getting a job at a pharmacy or pharmaceutical company or hospital?" Codie asked. "That way you'd gain experience in your chosen industry. Bartending can teach you some great communication skills, but wouldn't it be even better if you were contributing to your long-term career goals?"

"Well," the girl replied, "my cousin told me I have to go back to school and get a master's degree before I can get a pharmaceutical job."

"The good news is you can start working in your desired industry right now," Codie said. "Instead of spending two years in a job that won't advance your career, you could already be making progress toward your goals."

This had never occurred to her, and nobody had ever told her, so she was wasting her time in a job that had nothing to do with her real dream. Sadly, her story isn't unique.

Why spend your twenties gaining experience in the wrong industry or doing work that won't have any application to your career in your thirties and forties? Why tread water when you can be swimming mightily toward your desired destination?

WHAT WAS YOUR DREAM?

So what was your ninja billionaire dream when you were a little kid? When people used to ask you, "What do you want to be when you grow up?" how did you reply?

Do you remember how it used to feel when you gave people that answer? Does your dream look anything like your professional reality? Maybe you don't have a ninja billionaire dream. Maybe you have no idea where you belong or what you're supposed to do with your life. Or maybe you've already been through a bad launch and now you're trying to get back on track.

Whatever the case, we want to help you start moving toward the career that will bring you the most satisfaction. We want to give you a plan that will leverage your skills and interests for the next thirty to forty years. You don't have to wander through life with fingers crossed that you will finally land on some kind of work you don't hate.

All of this starts by creating a career-launch plan. To do that, we will help you identify your strengths so you can begin moving forward. Let's get started.

THE CAREER LAUNCH
MINDSET

When you run after every opportunity, you risk missing out on the right opportunity.

—ALAN NEWCOMB

We had a former student—we'll call him Alex—who came to us a few months after he'd launched his career. His first job position was perfect for the career path he wanted to take. It was in the right industry and gave him the opportunity to develop exactly the right skills and experience.

However, Alex told us, "I don't think this job is going to work out. I have to quit."

When we asked him what the problem was, we found his answer mind-boggling.

"I'm not sure I like my manager," he said. "We're just not connecting very well."

"This position is perfect for your career plans," we said. "It will take you exactly where you want to go."

"Yeah, but my manager doesn't seem to like me anymore," he replied.

As we discovered, he had been going around telling anyone who would listen that his manager sucked. It was a small company and a close-knit industry. Word had no doubt gotten back to the manager, who had responded in kind.

The Launcher was damaging his own career launch simply because his first boss wasn't quite what he wanted. In the process, he was also possibly shutting other doors in the industry. It was a perfect opportunity for his long-term goals, but he wanted his on-the-job experience to be perfect from day one. When it wasn't, he immediately began sabotaging his future.

Remember, a career launch requires patience because getting where you want to go takes time and commitment. It's a long-term plan.

REJECTING THE RIGHT OPPORTUNITY

One of our Launchers got a job interview at a great company. She had done a thorough job of selecting a company that matched her interests, and she was well prepared for the interview. We were excited to find out how it went, so we visited with her afterward.

"They offered me a job, and I accepted it," she told us.

"That's fantastic," we said. "Congratulations!"

"Thanks," she replied, "but I'm still looking for a better job."

We were stunned. "You're still looking for a better job even though you already accepted a job?"

"Yeah," she said. "I talked to my mom and dad, and they encouraged me to keeping looking."

"But you already told the company you would work for them."

"Well yeah, that's true," she said, "but I think the company knows I might not take it."

"How do they know that?" we asked.

The Launcher shrugged. "Doesn't every company know that?"

This mentality is the reason some Launchers accept as many job interviews as possible. We find that Launchers will sometimes send out résumés to a hundred different companies, even though only a fraction of them are a good fit because they believe that's what you're supposed to do.

Scheduling twenty interviews with twenty companies is a waste of time—your time and the company's time. Time is a precious resource for HR managers, CEOs, and other company leaders, so we recommend never taking a real job interview simply as practice. It's not fair to them or to you, particularly with their busy schedules.

Don't jump at every interview that comes along. Let your interests, needs, personality, and strengths drive your choices. Look for job opportunities that are a good fit for *you*. The best job hunting might involve only four or five interviews, but they are *targeted* interviews.

Another student came to our office to discuss her career situation. She was working a part-time job and had an opportunity to quit and work somewhere else. During our discussion, she said, "I have a lot more skills than the current job will let me use."

She further explained that she had worked part-time during her summer breaks in her father's successful, well-established business. As we discussed her long-term goals, it became clear that her father's company provided an excellent opportunity to use her skills and acquire the right experience.

When we asked her if she would ever be willing to work for him, she said, "I don't want to work for my family. I want to make my career my own."

Our response was, "Why not take advantage of your family's experience in business, especially if it will benefit your career plan? It's no different than taking advantage of your own strengths and skills."

What all of these examples reveal is the importance of developing *the right mindset* before you establish your launch criteria and put a plan together. To help you get there, we recommend the following two principles.

1) BE WILLING TO USE ALL OF YOUR SKILLS AND ADVANTAGES

You must understand and be willing to use all of your personal skills and every advantage in your career launch. This includes your personality traits and strengths, personal connections, and any experience you've acquired. Don't dismiss anything that might give you an edge.

2) COMMIT TO INCREASE YOUR EMOTIONAL INTELLIGENCE

Emotional intelligence is defined as "the capacity to be aware of, control, and express one's emotions, and to handle interpersonal relationships judiciously and empathetically."[1] We believe it is of foundational importance to any successful career launch, so as you begin to develop your career launch plan, consider working on increasing your emotional intelligence. It will influence every interaction you have as you seek, accept, and begin your career.

With high emotional intelligence, you will gain the ability to understand yourself and how you respond to different situations. You will begin to understand how other people think and feel, what drives them, and how they might respond to you. We will deal with emotional intelligence throughout this book, since it plays a key role in so much of your career.

---

1   Rose Leadem, "Why Emotional Intelligence Is Crucial for Success (Infographic),"
     Entrepreneur, August 12, 2018, https://www.entrepreneur.com/article/318187

DELIVERABLES TO SELF

Now it's time to commit to developing an actual career launch plan. Abandon this all-too-common notion that you're just going to stumble into your career, taking any old job that comes along, or choosing a career for reasons that won't advance your long-term goals. To do that, you have to take an emotionally intelligent approach to your career launch, which we'll look at in greater detail next.

As a personal exercise, we recommend having a serious conversation with yourself about your situation—skills, experience, personality, advantages—so you can figure out exactly what you want.

Spend a little time each day thinking about your career. If you're going to spend thirty or forty years in your career, isn't it worth a small part of each day? This daily thought exercise will help you keep and clarify what you want.

3

THE EMOTIONALLY INTELLIGENT CAREER LAUNCH PLAN

We find that parents have three primary goals for their adult children. First, they want you to be happy. Second, they want you to have a good job. Third, they want you to be able to afford a nice life for yourself. Unfortunately, we find that they are sometimes guilty of short-sighted thinking. For example, a parent might say, "Wow, you're making fifty thousand dollars a year. That's fantastic. You made it!"

Building a career is about so much more than just being satisfied with your entry-level salary. While your entry-level salary might sound great, if you're still making that much in ten or twenty years, you're going to be struggling to live a good life. Will you be able to afford nice cars, a nice house, vacations for your family, and all of the other things you dream about? You have to build toward something, which means planning for a long-term career.

AUNT SUSIE STANDARDS

During a meeting with a student, he mentioned that he had the opportunity to work as an actuarial at an insurance company—a job that was well outside of his skillset, personality, and career aspirations. When he told us he was seriously considering it, we asked him why.

"Well, my Aunt Susie worked as an actuarial for that same insurance company," he said. "My parents think I should take it because Aunt Susie made a lot of money and had a nice house."

Often, parents measure success for their children according to what we call "Aunt Susie" standards: a nice house, a decent spouse, a couple of cars, relatively good health. They might push Launchers to take a job that doesn't fit with their skills, experience, or personality because they've seen other people—possibly close family members, maybe even themselves—achieve some measure of financial success in that specific career field.

We're all familiar with the stereotype of the domineering parent who insists their children become either a doctor or a lawyer. When parents do this, even in subtle ways, they're not thinking about what's *right* for the Launcher; they're thinking about what will provide a decent living. Just because you're good at something does not mean you must do it, especially if it doesn't fulfill you.

We see a similar phenomenon with Relaunchers. Occasionally, Relaunchers will enter a career field that interests them and then leave it after a few months or years because a loved one says, "No, you should have gone into this other industry. It pays a lot better. Look at how well your Aunt Susie did at her job."

This is where emotional intelligence starts to become so important. You have to know yourself well so you don't end up pursuing a career that offers a "decent" salary, but is a horrible fit for you. Although their intentions are good, loved ones don't know your true desires and motivations.

We don't want to sound like we're being negative toward parents. Having parents who love and support you in your decisions is so important, and Launchers have every reason to be grateful when their parents want the best for them. However, a parent's love-blinded guidance can sometimes conflict with your long-term career goals, and if you don't know yourself very well, those conflicting goals might hinder your successful career launch.

One of the reasons we strongly recommend developing a mentor partnership is that a mentor in your preferred career field can help you see past the biases that have been instilled in you by parents and loved ones. Since a mentor is much closer to the workplace environment where you will end up, they can more effectively help you create a path for yourself.

We will address mentors in more detail in a later chapter, but for now, let's look at the specific steps for putting your career-launch plan together.

STEP ONE: COMMIT TO YOUR CAREER LAUNCH

Change is never easy, and your career launch represents one of the biggest and most dramatic changes you will experience in your life.

Think about the adjustment you experienced when you returned to college classes after summer break. Getting back into a full-time class schedule is often difficult. You spend the summer taking it easy or maybe working a part-time job or doing an internship. Maybe you even take a few summer classes, but when the fall semester rolls around, it always takes a couple of weeks to adjust and get back into the swing of a full-time class schedule.

A career launch is an even bigger and more dramatic transition. It's not something you can begin thinking about *after* graduation. On the contrary, in our experience, a career launch done correctly could take as long as six months. The same goes for relaunching a career. If you're not careful, those months can become a long, scary time when you're not earning any money.

We see many young adults using their parents as a last resort. They graduate and aren't ready to launch their career—or the first career fails, and they need to relaunch—so they move back home. We've never met a student who willingly went home and lived on their parents' couch, but sometimes they simply see no other options. This doesn't have to happen, but if you want to successfully launch or relaunch your career, the very first thing you need to do is *commit to the hard work.*

You are going to spend a lot of time and effort preparing for your career. We tell undergraduate students that it typically takes *at least as much work* as a regular three-credit college class, meaning three hours a week for fourteen weeks. That adds up to 2,100 minutes of actual class time, but when you factor in study and homework, it can run as high as 105 hours. To make it a little easier to remember, let's call it a "100-hour effort." That's what it will take to successfully prepare for your career.

We want you to be successful. We want you to identify what you value and how you want to live your life, but you have to make up your mind to devote enough time and effort to make it happen.

STEP TWO: CONSIDER THE COMPANY CULTURE

When thinking about your future career, it's important to think about the company culture that you want to be part of. You're going to get multiple job offers, and you have to look beyond the salary and specific benefits. Dive into the culture of the company to see if it's going to be a good fit.

We had a student named Julia who wanted to apply for a position at an insurance company. The particular company she chose is a fantastic place to work, but they have a "work hard and play hard" mentality. It's not uncommon for them to have a seventy-hour work week, but they spend a lot of that time networking and socializing with clients. The alcohol flows freely, and people have a good time.

We knew Julia didn't drink. In fact, she'd never had a single alcoholic beverage in her entire life and probably never will, because she's not comfortable around alcohol or people who drink. As a result, it was clear that this opportunity might not be a good fit for her.

She asked us, "Should I apply for this position?"

When we asked her about the company culture, she admitted that she would be miserable working in such an environment.

Even though it was a great company, we told her, "No, avoid it completely." After all, at the end of the day, we all want to fit in.

It's possible you've never actually thought about the kind of company culture you want to be part of. Culture is not simply the beliefs of company leaders. It also encompasses the expectations that are placed on employees. We will talk about the culture of your launch space in more detail in Chapter Four because it's one of the biggest causes of career launch failure!

STEP THREE: DEVELOP APPROPRIATE LAUNCH EXPECTATIONS

We find that many Launchers have misguided expectations due to society about their role as a new hire. Start setting realistic expectations *now* so you won't be disappointed in the future. If you're between twenty-one and

thirty-five, you've grown up in an age of instant gratification, and no career is instantly gratifying. It takes time
to acquire all of the great things you want and expect in
your career. This is so important that we've dedicated
a whole chapter to it. In Chapter Five, we will delve
deeply into career expectations so you can begin making
mental adjustments.

At the same time, in this age of social media, we're all
used to seeing people post positive things about their
lives, so it can feel like everyone in the world is living a
perfect life, except you. Your friends and acquaintances
are constantly taking fabulous vacations, eating amazing food, smiling and laughing and having a great time.
Yes, every once in a while, someone will post about a
tragedy, but that kind of post is the exception, not
the rule.

In a similar way, when companies are recruiting, they
mostly share only the positive aspects about working for
them. What about the more frustrating aspects of starting
a career: creating and living on a budget, paying bills, and
getting to work early in the morning every day, waiting
to earn vacation days? There are a lot of adjustments to
make, and it's possible that no one has ever sat down with
you and showed you how to deal with all of the frustrations that come with a new career. We want to provide
the guidance you've been looking for.

STEP FOUR: DEVELOP CAREER LAUNCH CRITERIA

Your launch criteria are based on your skills, personality traits, and aspirations. You can't evaluate any job offer until you've established these criteria and weighted them. Remember, *your* career launch is not like anyone else's career launch. In Chapter Six, we will give you a structured way to define your launch criteria so you can find the industry, company, and position that is perfectly suited for you (and vice versa).

In our experience, a career launch without clear criteria will be suboptimal at best, so you will want to think about the aspects of a career that will contribute to your idea of success.

STEP FIVE: INVENTORY YOUR SKILLS AND EXPERIENCE

The fifth step is to inventory your skills and experience so you know *exactly* what you have to offer. In order to identify the right career and company, in order to interview well, you must understand what you bring to the table (and what you *don't* bring). To do that, you have to know yourself very well—your desires, interests, experience, talents, skills, and knowledge.

You want to be able to sell yourself in interviews. You are also protecting yourself from getting into a situation where you are out of your area of capacity. For example, if you know you're not good at analyzing a large amount of data, you probably want to avoid a position that will require you to do this.

Graham Weston, the founder of Rackspace, is the benefactor of our sales program at Texas A&M, and we like to bring him to class from time to time to speak to our students. It's their chance to meet and hear from someone who has built an impressive legacy of career achievement, and for many students, it will be the first time they've ever spoken to a billionaire. When he speaks to the students, he always shares with them all of the things he's *not* good at.

"I'm very unorganized," he will say. "My desk is cluttered. I need other people to help me organize tasks because I can't do it by myself."

In fact, he even hired an organization coach in an effort to improve his organizational skills. As hard as he tried to keep his desk clear every day and never touch an email more than once, Graham eventually knew he was just never going to excel in organization.

We believe it's important for students to realize that a very successful person has some areas of weakness. You can acknowledge your imperfections, the things you're not good at, and your flaws and weaknesses without being discouraged by them. In Graham's case, his strengths and skills more than make up for them. For example, he is highly skilled at recognizing a good business deal and making timely strategic decisions.

Maybe you're not even sure what you bring to the table. It's surprising how little we know about ourselves. In Chapter Seven we will correct that, helping you identify exactly what you have to offer.

THE SEVEN CAREER COMPETENCIES

Once you've followed these steps, we believe there are *seven career competencies* you have to learn or develop in order to successfully launch your career: *mentoring, interviewing, networking, job shadowing, professionalism, travel,* and *reading*. We will deal with each of them so that by the end of this book, you have a complete picture of the path ahead of you.

We've provided the following chart with behaviorally anchored ratings for each competency. This will help you start to get a clear sense of where you already stand on these core competencies. If you don't feel like you're ready to do this exercise now—if you don't feel like you know yourself well enough yet—come back to it later. Remember, we want this book to serve as a handbook that you can reference again and again throughout your career launch and into your career.

For each career competency, give yourself a rating between one and ten based on how well you think you are doing *right now* in this particular area. Once you've rated each of your career competencies, add up each one to get an overall score. We believe this number should be at least a fifty (out of a possible seventy) before you're ready to consider launching your career. If you're not there yet, don't despair. In the early stages of your career launch, you might be closer to twenty or thirty, but we're going to help you move closer to that magic number of fifty.

EVALUATING YOUR CAREER COMPETENCIES.

DATE OF COMPLETION _____

Select your position on each scale, then add up your total career competencies score for all seven categories.

Mentoring
(Chapter 9)

0_0_ 1__ 2__	3__ 4__ 5__	6__ 7__ 8__ 9__	10__ (Current Score)
no mentors selected	one mentor selected	mentor council created	mentor council created and met with all mentors

Interviewing
(Chapter 10)

0__ 1__ 2__	3_0_ 4__ 5__	6__ 7__ 8__ 9__	10__ (Current Score)
no practice interviews		three practice interviews	four or more practice interviews with video review and evaluation

Networking
(Chapter 11)

0__ 1__ 2__	3__ 4✔ 5__	6__ 7✔ 8__ 9__	10__ (Curre
zero to three professionals		twenty professionals	fifty or more professionals

Job Shadowing
(Chapter 12)

0✔ 1__ 2__	3__ 4__ 5__	6__ 7__ 8__ 9__	10__ (Current Score)
no job shadow experience	at least three job shadows	seven or eight job shadows	ten or more job shadows with structured review

Professionalism
(Chapter 13)

0__ 1__ 2__	3__ 4__ 5__	6__ 7__ 8__ 9__	10_✔ (Current Score)
no experience in a professional setting	cocktail parties or other casual settings		professional meetings with company professionals

Travel
(Chapter 14)

0__ 1__ 2__	3__ 4__ 5__	6__ 7✔ 8__ 9__	10__ (Current Score)
no travel outside local community	extensive travel in home state	extensive travel in the United States	international travel

Reading
(Chapter 15)

0__ 1✔ 2__	3__ 4__ 5__	6__ 7__ 8__ 9__	10__ (Current Score)
no professional business reading	two or three books read	five or more books read	nine or more books read

FINAL ADVICE

In the final chapters of this book, we will provide some additional expertise and experience. Sometimes, a job simply doesn't work out, so in Chapter Seventeen, we will look at some criteria that can help you decide when it's time to move on. As we like to say, keep your parachute packed so you can land safely, but don't jump until the conditions are right.

Chapter Eighteen is perhaps the most unique chapter in the book. In the workplace, you're going to find yourself working alongside Gen Xers and baby boomers, two generations with different perspectives and experiences. The differences are most stark between baby boomers and millennials, so we want to provide some advice to help you navigate these differences. While our advice won't solve every problem, it will give you a perspective and some effective solutions for many common generational problems.

Finally, in the last chapter, we will look at creating your own personal brand, discussing all of the individual components that define how the professional world perceives you. By the end, you will hopefully have a crystal clear overview of the road ahead so you can approach your career launch with confidence.

THE CULTURE OF YOUR LAUNCH SPACE (THIS IS ABOUT *YOU*)

A student from our program accepted a position at a chemical company on the East Coast. As we helped her prepare for her launch, we considered the alignment of her skills with her specific launch space. In the process, we noticed she'd earned two Ds in chemistry in college.

In our sales program, we always tell students, "We will teach you sales skills, but you have to bring the science you need." We spoke to the Launcher about this potential misalignment, but she was convinced it was the right opportunity. Two weeks after she started working for the company, her manager dumped six big chemistry books on her desk and said, "There are some important things you can glean from these books to develop your professional skills. Read them and learn from them." Then he dumped a couple more books and said, "These are the reference materials for our specific chemical products, so read these as well and be sure you understand them thoroughly."

They had her take the books to a conference room, then shut the door behind her. After two weeks in that conference room, she reached a breaking point. Crying, she left work, understanding very little of what she'd read about chemistry, the company, or their products.

Eight weeks after she started working there, her boss tested her knowledge of the company's chemical products. She failed miserably, and the company threatened to fire her. Her boss called Dr. Litzenberg and said, "Look, Doc, you have to do some warranty work on your student here. She's simply unable to learn the chemistry."

It's not unusual for us to talk to alumni of our program or their bosses after they start working, especially if something is going wrong. As with this book, we like to journey with people into their careers and make sure they have what they need to be successful. As part of that ongoing help, we sometimes do what we call "warranty work" when a student proves to be a mismatch to a company culture or launch space.

In this case, our former student was miserable. We met with her and discussed her situation, and she decided to leave the chemical firm. She found a career at a different kind of firm where the requisite skills and products she handled didn't require much knowledge of chemistry. It was a better fit, and she found the work much more rewarding and satisfying. Thanks to her successful relaunch, she has enjoyed a highly successful eighteen-year career.

As our mentor and benefactor Graham Weston loves to say, "We all want to be valued members of a winning team on an inspiring mission." We love that saying so much that it's mounted on the wall in our office. It's also an important truth that we see again and again in the lives of the students we work with. It's as true for Launchers as it is for Relaunchers. To reach that point, you're going to have to understand the culture of your launch space. Let's take a look at a few aspects of your launch space that might require some significant adjustment.

AUTONOMY AND THE LACK OF FEEDBACK

Although you can't control whether an individual company or the economy itself is doing well—and you certainly can't prevent another recession from happening—there are many aspects of your launch space that are entirely within your control. For example, you get to decide the specific industry or area of specialization you look into.

Remember, the culture of your career launch is very different from the culture of being a student. You probably already know and expect that, but many Launchers aren't prepared for just how profound the differences are. As a student, you experienced constant evaluation. Every assignment received a grade, and you had quizzes and tests along the way so you maintained a clear sense of how you were doing.

In the career space, you don't get reviewed very often, not in a way that's similar to a semester grade. As a student, if you studied hard and aced your quizzes, your high grades provided constant positive feedback, but in a professional environment, you might not get more than an annual review. You might not get any regular feedback at all. This creates a very different reward system.

At the same time, you might struggle with the greater degree of autonomy in the workplace. You don't have to ask someone if you want to be excused from the room to take a phone call. Most of the time, you just get up and go. This might sound like a minor thing, but some Launchers struggle with it. They've gotten used to asking for permission for so many things throughout their lives.

The difference can feel like a "sink or swim" situation if you're not prepared for it.

When Launchers come to us after they start working and say, "I'm not happy working for this company," the vast majority of the time it's because their personality and needs don't match well with the company culture. For example, we had a Launcher who needed constant feedback. In class, he would ask us three or four times a week, "How am I doing in class?" We knew if he wound up with a manager who was very hands-off, who essentially said, "Do your own thing, and I'll let you know if something's wrong," he would struggle. To thrive, he needed a company culture in which leadership remained actively involved with the team's performance.

Later, we will talk about the nature of work travel. Some companies require their employees to travel regularly for work purposes, while other companies never send their employees anywhere outside of the office. Some Launchers love the idea of getting to travel to different places on the company's dime, and they may even want to travel internationally. Others will find it a grueling test of endurance.

In some companies, it's normal to work sixty to seventy hours a week chasing clients, so if you expect to work forty hours a week, you're going to struggle. You need to investigate the culture of any company that makes you an offer so you know if you will be a good match. Don't set yourself up for failure.

BALANCING YOUR BUDGET

Most Launchers have little experience with creating and living by a budget. Maybe you haven't yet had to pay your own bills. Like many students, your parents might have supported you financially while you lived on campus. This is perfectly normal, but it means you might not yet know what it's like to find an apartment and pay the utilities and other bills every month.

Be sure to consider your personal budget when you receive a salary offer so you know you can pay your bills and still live your life. Sometimes, Launchers have unrealistic expectations about the kind of lifestyle they will be able to live when they begin their careers.

During a school trip to France, Dr. Litzenberg was staying with a group of students from our program a few hundred miles from Paris. One weekend, he took the students on a bus trip into Paris to see the sights. A student sitting next to him was talking about her boyfriend, and she said, "I'm sure he's going to meet us in Paris this weekend. I can just see him catching up with us under the Eiffel Tower and asking me to marry him, as he whips out a two-carat diamond ring. Can you imagine that? It wouldn't surprise me."

Dr. Litzenberg knew her boyfriend worked at a grocery store, and there was no way he could afford to take a week off work and pay for a flight to Paris just to meet her under the Eiffel Tower, much less buy her a twenty-five thousand dollar diamond ring. He hadn't worked long enough to save the money to afford it, and he probably didn't have the credit. The student had very unrealistic expectations when it came to money.

This isn't unusual with Launchers. We find they often have unrealistic expectations about the kind of lifestyle their entry-level salary is going to afford them. "I'll buy a nice house, a new car, and I'll take so many cool vacations." The simple truth is you can't afford all of those things on an entry-level salary, not in the beginning. Regular expenses will consume most of your income.

When considering your launch space, you have to make sure your expectations line up with a healthy personal budget. Are you going to be paying student loans? What other bills will you be paying? We recommend creating an Excel spreadsheet and working out your personal post-graduation budget. Include things like rent and utilities, student loans, groceries, gas, and other vehicle expenses, possibly a gym membership, as well as any ongoing health-care costs. When you receive an offer from a company, you will then have some idea of how much money is left over after paying all of your bills. However, this isn't money to just burn through. We strongly encourage you to begin putting a little of this money into savings and a 401(k) right away, so you won't struggle financially in the future.

CHANGING FAMILY RELATIONSHIPS

We find that some students want to move back to their hometown and live close to their family as soon as they graduate. While that's perfectly fine, it creates severe limitations on a career launch. Often, to make it happen, Launchers accept a low-paying job close to home that they are way overqualified for.

If you want to launch yourself into a truly successful career that aligns with your skills, experience, and long-term career goals, you will probably have to accept that your proximity with your family is going to change. You might not have as much social interaction with them as you used to, and you probably won't receive the same amount of monetary support or parental guidance. While you might want to live across the street from your parents in your hometown, your career might draw you away to another city or state.

The good news is that if you pursue a successful career

and create a healthy budget, you will have money to fly home from time to time and visit your loved ones. Nevertheless, it requires a bit of a mental adjustment to accept the fact that you probably won't be located close to your family. The nature of your relationship with siblings, parents, and other loved ones is going to change.

Even when you get married and have a family of your own, it's best to maintain a realistic view of how your career will impact those relationships. We had a student call us and complain, "My firm expects me to be at work at 8 a.m. on Friday morning. How can I go out on dates with my spouse like we always do on Thursday nights if I have to be at work that early on Friday morning?"

Let's be clear, we are committed to spending time with our families, and we always want to respond quickly to any needs or emergencies that our own loved ones have. In fact, one of the things we love about our current positions is that we have just enough flexibility to be available for our families. However, your career space is going to make demands of your family and personal time, so time management will become very important.

If you have a family priority that takes place at three p.m. every day, you can either try to find a career environment that allows you to meet that obligation, have a conversation with a boss, or accept that your job won't allow it, in which case a spouse might have to take care of it. You can't simply decide to leave work in the middle of the afternoon for a personal priority. If you need to take some time off for an important family event, you have to ask for time off, and you may need to ask well in advance.

Last year, we planned a fun activity for Launchers on Labor Day, and we just had one of our Launchers call to tell us he couldn't make it. He is working in a retail environment, and it wasn't a good idea for him to ask for time off on a busy shopping day. It would have created extra stress for his team and wouldn't have earned him any points with his bosses, so he made a smart choice.

If you end up in a retail environment, you will have similar holiday demands on your time that you will have to work around with loved ones. For example, Christmas Eve is a day when many shoppers purchase last-minute gifts. While people in other industries might take that day off and relax with family, you can expect to work extra hard. You can always spend the same amount of quality time with your loved ones on a different day.

Ultimately, you have to identify and understand the culture you're stepping into so you can create realistic expectations about how it will affect your personal relationships. Figure out what's important to you before you get yourself into a situation that is unworkable. Think about things like holidays, time off, travel, vacation time, and work hours. Be realistic, but find something that fits with your personal needs.

Maybe you love taking vacations to exotic locations more than you love buying expensive items. Do you have realistic expectations about what your work schedule and available vacation time will actually allow? Dr. Litzenberg now earns four weeks of vacation a year, but there's simply no way he can be away for four weeks without falling behind on his responsibilities.

WHAT ARE YOUR EXPECTATIONS?

When it comes to the culture of your launch space, you must understand what you're getting into. Life is going to be different in many ways, but we believe developing your emotional intelligence will go a long way in helping you make a successful transition into your chosen workplace.

EMOTIONALLY INTELLIGENT EXPECTATIONS

The world is full of graduates who think they deserve a job.

—TRENT BISHOP, VP OF SALES FOR LONE STAR CITRUS

One of the biggest contributing factors to a happy and satisfying career is setting the right expectations for your career launch. This is where emotional intelligence comes into play since emotional intelligence is about understanding yourself and others. In particular, it's about understanding the ways in which you (and others) respond to various circumstances, events, and stimuli. There are many different emotional stimuli that affect our career satisfaction and lives, and there are many emotional stimuli that impact our career decisions. For example, we all react in different ways to the stimulus of money.

Students come to us with certain expectations about money that have already been instilled in them by their families or the circumstances they experienced growing up. They have specific ideas about budgeting, saving, investing, debt, and spending on things like children, pets, vehicles, and vacations, and these ideas are all emotional triggers that solicit emotional responses.

Understanding these stimuli and your responses to them are part of emotional intelligence. We've had students say things like, "I will never take out a mortgage on a house because then I will have payments for fifteen to thirty years." This is an expectation that has been instilled in them somewhere along the way, and we have to remind them that sixty-five percent of homes in the United States have a mortgage on them.[2] Furthermore, very few Launchers will have three-hundred thousand dollars in checking to pay cash for a house.

If your career launch takes you somewhere like California or New York, you should expect to have a sizeable mortgage payment at some point. It will be a large part of

---

2   Christopher Ingraham, "How Many Families Actually Own Half-Million-Dollar Homes?" *Washington Post*, November 3, 2017, https://www.washingtonpost.com/news/wonk/wp/2017/11/03/how-many-families-actually-own-half-million-dollar-homes.

your budget, even if you settle for a modest home. However, even in a low-cost housing state like Texas, you will still need $250,000 for a reasonable home, which means you'll need a mortgage. That's a realistic expectation.

RECOGNIZING YOUR TRIGGERS

Because of your family, upbringing, background, and experiences, you have some specific emotional triggers that cause you respond to certain situations in particular ways. Your emotional responses are unique to you, and becoming emotionally intelligent means, first of all, recognizing these triggers. The way you *respond* to these emotional triggers is also a component of emotional intelligence. Fortunately, you are not enslaved to your emotional triggers, so when you understand yourself, you can choose how you want to respond.

The amygdala in your brain produces fear, anxiety, and aggression, and if you're not self-aware, your behavior will be led by these emotions. Maybe when you go out on Friday night and have a little too much to drink, someone bumps into you, and your alcohol-compromised amygdala starts telling you to get into a fight. You have to learn how to recognize this so you can learn to control your response. Just because your amygdala says to fight doesn't mean you can't *choose* to find a more rational way to resolve the situation.

One of our top students, Grant, got a nice job selling software for a top-notch firm with an outstanding training program. In fact, their five-year training program is so highly rated that some people will get a job there just to go through the learning experience, because it prepares them for a highly successful career in the industry.

Grant, on the other hand, lasted about five months before he called us and said, "I think I have to quit. I'm just not making any impact in the company. I don't feel like my contribution matters." In a large company like that, new recruits are often used for customer service, even if their position will ultimately move full time into software development, training, or sales. Grant was dealing with up to forty customer service calls a day, and from his vantage point, sitting in a little cubicle, he felt like his skills and time were being wasted.

"I think I'll look for a job in the medical devices industry instead," he said. "I think I'd like it better there."

His short-term frustration was understandable, but staying long term at the company would certainly have benefited his career goals. Sitting in a little cubicle and answering the phones all day was triggering a negative emotional response, and Grant's amygdala was screaming, "Get out of here!" Because of the emotional response, he assumed his job was a bad fit, and he began to look for a quick exit. He saw the medical devices industry as an escape, and he romanticized it in his mind, even though he'd never done any job shadowing in that industry.

We counseled him to stick with his job for at least two years so he could get past the "new recruit" phase and begin to experience what the job was really going to be like long term. After all, there was no guarantee that he'd do any better in the medical devices industry, and his current position was perfect for his idea of long-term goals, even though he couldn't specifically define those goals. To stay and endure the customer service calls, Grant had to *choose* to act contrary to his deep-seated emotional responses.

If you understand your own emotional triggers, you can recognize when they are attempting to influence your behavior in a way that will hinder your career. More importantly, you can choose to act differently.

SHORT-TERM DISAPPOINTMENT

The impact you make and the value you bring as a new recruit won't necessarily be obvious at first. You're not going to be steering the ship after three weeks on the job, and you're not going to be the CEO overnight. You're going to have to be there for a while before you feel like your contribution is noticeable. A successful career takes time, so let go of any desire for instant gratification. *Be patient!* Don't let short-term disappointment get in the way of your long-term goals. In order for you to see your impact, you're going to have to make an investment. Many Launchers think that their impact should be obvious after six months, but we think it takes more like two years. Companies expect you to start somewhere close to zero. Making an impact takes time, but you'll never get there if you don't practice patience.

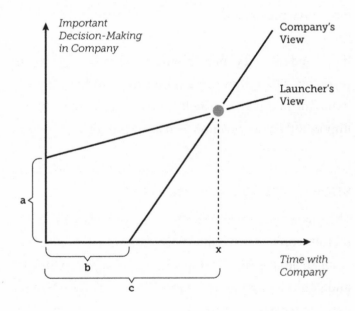

A LAUNCHER'S VIEW OF THEIR STRATEGIC VALUE FOR DECISION-MAKING PURPOSES COMPARED TO THE COMPANY'S VIEW

In this graph, we have a Launcher's view of their strategic value for decision-making purposes compared to the company's view. This is sometimes a great source of frustration for Launchers. Launchers assume they will have substantial value to the decision-makers of a company at the onset of their employment [a], a view that begins immediately upon employment [time 0] and increases over time (as indicated by the Launcher's view line). Companies, on the other hand, assume it will take a new hire some amount of time [b] to learn about the company before they can contribute significantly to decision-making, which will then increase over time [View of Company line].

The two views cross at point x. For the time period before x, the Launcher's view indicates that they believe they should have more impact on company decision-making than the company thinks they should have. To put it another way, until a Launcher has been with a company for total time [c], the company believes they have less impact on decision-making than the Launcher does.

The end result of these differing views is that Launchers are often frustrated by what they perceive as a lack of respect from the company. For example, a fast-track Launcher might assume they're ready to represent their company in international negotiations well before company leaders will allow it.

We've had several Launchers quit over miscommunication about the amount of impact they would have in a company. One former student launched his career at an international firm with over three-hundred thousand employees, but he quit after five months because the company failed to implement his suggestions. This was a loss for both the company and the Launcher.

For this reason, it's best to make sure your expectations as a Launcher are realistic in light of company practices and policies. We strongly encourage you to learn a company's practices and policies from a company-level mentor. This will help you avoid this kind of miscommunication.

Just because you have an education doesn't mean you will be handed an awesome job with awesome responsibilities right after graduation. Often, people expect to walk into a job fair or career expo, stumble into the right person, and get a perfect job offer that fulfills every need and desire from day one.

The percentage of Launchers who launch their career at a job fair is very low. Those kinds of events are better for creating relationships and meeting industry people. To find a good career fit, you're probably going to have to spend some time looking for it. That's one reason why it's so important not to wait until you graduate to start looking. You're probably not going to step down off the podium, diploma in hand, and be met by some company executive who says, "Congratulations, we have the perfect job for you doing exactly what you want."

It is likely that you will not get hired into midlevel management right out of the gate. We have Launchers who take management courses, and they expect to be managing people from day one, despite the fact that they have no actual experience. You have to learn to *be* managed before you can manage others.

Don't expect to be the boss right away. Companies are smarter than that. In fact, don't even *ask* to be a manager until you've paid your dues. They're going to offer you an entry-level position. Not everybody loves an entry-level position, but that's how you get into the workforce. Don't worry about your title. We all want to have a badge that says "Director of Marketing" or some other impressive thing that looks great when posted on social media, but strategic advancement takes time. You started from the bottom. Now you're here! The reward is well worth it.

NOBODY WILL HOLD YOUR HAND

Your boss won't have time to give you constant feedback and affirmation. Bosses have more important things to focus on, so learn to appreciate yourself. Thrive off your own self-satisfaction at your progress and achievement. Track your own measurable growth. Then, when you meet with your boss, you can share those things. "Here are the things I've accomplished in the past six months."

In the professional world, nobody will hold your hand. Your company will guide you to some degree, but they're not going to tell you exactly what to do hour by hour. Mentally and emotionally prepare yourself for this level of responsibility and autonomy. You will have deadlines, but you will have to set your own agenda to meet them.

Dr. Litzenberg assigns a major project to students every semester and gives them a specific deadline. If they turn it in a week late, he takes off ten points. If they turn it in two weeks late, he takes off twenty points. If they turn it in three weeks late, they get a zero.

Though he makes the rules very clear, he still has students walk into his office five weeks late and try to turn in their project. "I know this is a little late," they'll say, "so I guess you'll have to take off a few points." They expect the deadline to be flexible. In the professional world, deadlines are fixed and real, and Dr. Litzenberg's deadline is meant to reinforce this career reality.

If your boss says, "I'd like this done by two o'clock today," they don't mean you can come in next Monday at 4:30 p.m. He's not going to accept the assignment and simply take a few points off the final score. It's not flexible like some college assignments. It's real work at a real company affecting a real bottom line. Your job and your career aspirations are at stake. We don't say this lightly. Placing your own prioritization on an already prioritized to-do list could get you in a lot of trouble and risk your reputation.

This year, we had fifty-three of our students doing summer internships at various companies. On a Friday morning, one of those interns came to visit us in our office, and she said, "I have to talk to you about how badly the company treated me." We quickly learned that she'd been fired two weeks before the end of her internship.

When we asked her why she got fired, her first response was, "I was getting ready to quit anyway." We pressed her for more information, and she finally said, "They told us we were supposed to give our final presentation to corporate officers from Louisiana on Monday, but the officers couldn't make it, so they postponed the presentation until Tuesday. I couldn't make it on Tuesday, so I wasn't able to give my report."

"Why couldn't you make it on Tuesday?" we asked.

"I was moving into my new apartment," she said. "The apartment wasn't available until Monday night, so I had to move in on Tuesday."

She didn't see the importance of prioritizing the presentation, tabling her responsibilities outside of work, despite the fact that the executives to whom she was giving the presentation had a direct influence in deciding to offer her a full-time position upon graduation.

Sometimes a deadline won't even be stated explicitly. It will be implied. "Get this two-page summary of your financial evaluation finished and on my desk as soon as possible." That doesn't mean you can work at your leisure. Even if your boss doesn't give you a fixed date, it doesn't mean they won't be furious if you don't turn it in for two months when it should have taken two days. Feel free to ask, "How soon do you need this?"

Your boss isn't going to hold your hand, you won't get constant affirmation, and deadlines are going to matter. That's the new world you are stepping into, and you need to mentally prepare for it. You must begin setting realistic expectations for your career right now, long before your first day on the job.

GIVE IT TIME

Once you begin your career, you need to give it time. It will take at least eighteen months before you're able to truly evaluate the success of your career launch. We recommend measuring the job against your career launch criteria at the beginning and then every six months thereafter. By the time you get to your eighteenth month on the job, you will finally have a sense of whether or not you've made a mistake. If so, don't despair. It might be time for a relaunch.

It also takes time for you to feel like you know what you're doing. In fact, we think it can take anywhere from three to five *years* before you feel truly confident about the work you're doing. In his book *Outliers*, Malcolm Gladwell states that it takes about ten-thousand hours to become an expert at anything. While the ten-thousand-hour rule might not be hard and fast for everyone at every task, it at least reinforces the need for *patience*. Give it time. Learn the ropes. Gain confidence. Then you will know whether or not you've launched successfully.

When evaluating your career launch, be aware of something called impostor syndrome, a psychological pattern in which an individual doubts their accomplishments and has an internalized fear of being exposed as a fraud. Separate your feelings from facts to decipher whether or not your doubts are logical.

DELIVERABLES TO SELF

As a personal exercise, spend some time thinking about your own family, upbringing, background, and experiences. What are your expectations about things like money, deadlines, feedback, and professional relationships? Can you identify specific emotional triggers that cause you respond to certain situations in particular ways? Developing an awareness of your own emotional responses will be more important than ever as you approach your career launch.

RECOMMENDED READING

Emotional Intelligence by Daniel Goleman

Emotional Intelligence 2.0 by Travis Bradberry and Jean Greaves

Outliers: The Story of Success by Malcolm Gladwell

6

LAUNCH CRITERIA (I JUST WANT TO HAVE *FUN* AND *LOVE* MY JOB)

In order to evaluate job offers and find the right one, you first have to develop your launch criteria. We often find students struggling to choose between offers. "I have two possible jobs, and I have no idea which one to take."

When they say something like that, we always sit them down and say, "Let's figure out what you're really looking for."

In this chapter, we're going to help you create a weighted list of criteria that will help you find the right industry, company, and job offer. We believe this is one of the most important activities you must complete *before* you start looking for career opportunities. Developing your launch criteria can't be rushed. It's like a fine wine; it takes time to get it right.

We believe you need several weeks of constant evaluation and overhaul of your list before you begin to consider job offers. When we take students through this exercise, we usually have them develop their launch criteria at the beginning of the semester. If you are planning for a career launch in May, ideally you will have completed your launch criteria by Christmas. That means it's best to start developing your list in early fall.

How does it work? To put it simply, you're going to sit down and think about the criteria you will use personally to evaluate a job offer. Make a list of the things that matter to you (e.g., training, salary, potential for advancement, job responsibilities). Expect to have eight to ten items on your list.

Here's an example of what a table might look like, but don't copy this one. Use your own personal criteria:

LAUNCH CRITERIA SAMPLE TABLE

Training (Initial and Ongoing)
Salary
Potential for Pay Advancement
Potential for Advancement in Job Responsibility
Company Culture Match
Future of the Firm
Target Customer Match
Product/Product Science Match
Technology Match
Job Schedule Flexibility

In this sample table, our Launcher has selected the key criteria that he or she believes will matter most when evaluating a career opportunity. Now, it's time to create your own list. However, if you don't yet know what industry you want to work in, you need to stop and figure that out before taking this next step. The industry you choose should line up with your skills, experience, and personality.

SELECTING AN INDUSTRY

If you are still trying to decide what industry to go into, don't worry. You have a huge amount of information to process and sort through. First, consider what you're passionate about. Do you like the outdoors, sports, or possibly nonprofit work? Seek your areas of interest.

For example, we spoke to Merritt, a student earning her degree in human resource development. When evaluating companies, she contemplated applying for big corporations like PepsiCo and Oracle. During our conversation, it became clear that there was no spark when she spoke about these companies, so we asked her what she loved doing and what she did on the weekend or as hobbies. She told us she loved fishing, especially in the bay, so we encouraged her to apply for an HR position in a company like Daiwa or Savage Gear—companies that supply fishing gear to retail stores.

"That never even crossed my mind," she said.

She left feeling excited and hopeful about the possibility of getting a position in an industry she was passionate about. Sit back and ask yourself, "What am I passionate about? What do I love doing, and how can I make that into a career?"

SELECT YOUR CRITERIA

Once you have chosen an industry, you're ready to create your own career launch criteria. Think carefully about the criteria that matter most to you. Eventually, you are going to give a numerical value to each of the items on the list, but don't worry about that yet. For now, just write down the criteria in no particular order.

Once you're done, put your list away for at least a week while you are exploring other career-building principles.

When you bring it back out, think through your criteria again and make sure you didn't forget anything. At this point, you can get your mentors involved to help you think through your list.

If you're reading through this book for the first time, you may not have mentors yet. We will talk about developing a mentor council in Chapter Eight. Go ahead and create your launch criteria list, but hold on to it for the time being. Finish reading this chapter, but come back to it once you have your mentors, and then you can complete the exercise.

Ask your mentors what they like the most and the least about their own careers. Then show them your launch criteria list and get their feedback. When you've finished speaking to your mentors about your launch criteria, give a numeric ranking to each item on the list, making sure that the sum of all ratings adds up to a hundred. The higher the number, the more important an individual criterion is to you, so think about this step carefully.

In the past several years, we've had a few students who have accepted good job offers without first establishing a clear sense of their own launch criteria. Grant, who we mentioned earlier, was one of those students. As he approached graduation, finishing up his bachelor of science degree at Texas A&M, he was constantly looking for the "best" job offer. He finally accepted a premium position at a highly respected software company.

Unfortunately, he never took the time to develop a launch criteria list, so he didn't have a clear sense of what he wanted and valued most in a dream job. Consequently, within a few months of starting his job, he was already looking for a "better" job. Even though he was working at a nationally respected company with a long-standing positive reputation, Grant didn't enjoy the entry-level work. Since he didn't have a clear sense of what criteria mattered most to him, he found himself in this destructive mindset of obsessively looking for something better without having a good idea of what better would be.

David was another student who neglected this vital step. After a successful summer internship at a regional meat processing firm, he was offered a permanent position to begin at the end of the following spring semester. Since his career launch already seemed to be on track, he didn't feel like he needed to develop his launch criteria.

Sadly, just as the end of the spring semester approached, the company experienced a major financial crisis, and they contacted David to tell him they wouldn't be able to bring him on board. Because David had failed to develop his launch criteria, he was ill-prepared to start looking for another job, and with the spring semester coming to an end, most companies had ended their recruiting season.

PUTTING THINGS INTO PERSPECTIVE

Weighting your launch criteria can help you put some of your on-the-job frustrations into perspective once you begin working for your chosen company. Jake became the number-one salesperson in his company, opening up new territories and helping his firm launch several new product lines as extensions of their core business. When we first helped him complete his launch criteria list, here's what he came up with:

JAKE'S LAUNCH CRITERIA LIST

Criteria	Weighting
Match with customers	30
Working in central Texas	20
Opportunity to do new things	20
Be in charge of my territory	20
Compensation in alignment with success	10
Total score should add up to 100	

A few years after Jake started working for the firm, we visited him to see how he was doing. Though he had excelled at the job, he expressed frustration with his compensation. He believed his pay didn't match his outstanding performance.

We pulled out Jake's launch criteria list and reminded him of the relatively low weight he'd given to "compensation in alignment with success." Either he had given it too low of a score, or he had simply responded too strongly to an emotional trigger over his pay. This helped him put his frustration into perspective and, ultimately, he realized he had simply responded to an emotional trigger about his salary compared to his peers. Compensation wasn't nearly as important to him as other aspects of his job.

LOVING YOUR JOB

Some students will put "I want to love my job" on their list of launch criteria and give it a heavy weight. Whether or not you're going to love your job is very hard to gauge until you've worked there for a while, so it's not a good criterion for evaluating job offers. Instead, identify the specific *aspects* of the job that might help you enjoy the environment you're in.

The old saying, "Choose a job you love, and you will never work a day in your life," has been attributed to Confucius. It has also been attributed to Mark Twain. Whatever its true origin, according to Malcolm Gladwell in *Outliers*, the concept of loving your job really didn't start to appear in newspaper, magazines, or social media until about 2000. It didn't become a common mentality until millennials began to enter the workforce.

Even in a job you enjoy, there are going to be days when

you *don't* love it. There will be hard work and frustration, and some days, you will go home exhausted. Ideally, you will enjoy your position, but you may not love it every day. Sometimes you will simply have to get down to work and endure the rough times. They do call it "work," after all, and not "play." Even if you wind up becoming a ninja billionaire, there are going to be days when being a ninja billionaire is hard, exhausting, and frustrating.

As a variant on this, some students will use the question, "What do I love to do?" to establish launch criteria. When we ask students what they love to do, the answers they give us aren't always things that are conducive to a good career.

We had a student answer the question by saying, "I love to ride horses."

There are perhaps fifty people around the Dallas area whose jobs allow them to be full-time horse trainers, so there simply aren't many opportunities to ride horses for a living. However, the student didn't stop there. He had a very precise ambition. He told us, "I want to become the executive director of the Texas Quarter Horse Association."

The current director of the Texas Quarter Horse Association probably has another twenty years left in his career. Even if that student could start a career working full time with quarter horses, rising to the level of executive director of a specific organization is going to take a very long time.

At the same time, if the student had managed to obtain his desired career, he would have been in for a rude awakening. Riding horses ten hours a day can be extremely tough, a much different experience than the occasional hour-long ride he was used to.

We're not closing the door completely to the possibility that a strange notion such as this can lead to an actual career. It is possible, though unlikely. For example, we had a student say, "I want to find a job where I can shoot guns all day long. Can you help me?"

We're always happy when students find luck into something, so to help him, we contacted a former student who works for an ammunition company. The Launcher wound up getting a job with them, and he now spends his days at trap-and-shoot events, helping people understand the value of his company's brand of ammunition.

Of course, this kind of unusual success depends on having mentors with industry connections who can point you in the right direction. We would have said this Launcher's career aspiration was silly if we hadn't had the connection to help him make it possible.

Still, his experience is the exception, not the rule. Occasionally, students luck into a job that satisfies some unusual personal preference, but it happens very rarely. However, if you use your career launch criteria, refer back to them from time to time, and get the right mentors, you greatly improve chances of finding a job you enjoy.

In most cases, we encourage students to use their hobbies to refuel during their downtime. Maybe they love walking their dog, or painting, or hanging out with friends, or running. Rather than making those things career goals, they can become a vital piece of the Launcher's self-care practices.

If you love cooking, you may not want to open your own restaurant. Running a restaurant is not very relaxing, but maybe cooking can become the activity that helps you unwind after a long day at work.

Your launch criteria list can serve as a constant reminder of what truly matters to you during those early months on the job. When you're going through a season of doubt or not having a good time, you can refer back to it and put things into perspective.

DELIVERABLES TO SELF

This chapter is *absolutely essential* to the success of your career launch. You can't skim over it and say, "I don't want to follow this step. I'll just go to the next thing." Without your launch criteria list, you won't be able to evaluate job offers effectively. If at all possible, sit down *right now* and start working on your list of criteria. *You have to get this step right!* You can use the fill-in-the-blank matrix we've provide in this chapter, or you can open an Excel spreadsheet.

Use brainstorming techniques to come up with your initial list of criteria. If you haven't done this before, it involves quickly writing down anything that comes to mind without regard to the wording. Remember, you're not weighting the criteria yet. You won't do that until after you've met with a mentor. Your mentor will help you think through these criteria and point you to opportunities that align with your list.

After you create your initial list, put it away for a week, then come back to it and evaluate your criteria. Make any adjustments that seem appropriate. You will revisit this list many times before and after your career launch, so keep it handy.

Remember, you're more likely to love your job if you do your due diligence on this step. Your list of criteria will

YOUR LAUNCH CRITERIA

(YOUR NAME _____ **)**

Criteria Weighting

1)

2)

3)

4)

5)

6)

7)

8)

9)

10)

Weightings should add up to a hundred

_____

Reserve this section for mentor feedback and additions.

help you evaluate each job offer, and it will help you keep things in perspective when you have rough days at work.

DO YOUR CRITERIA ALIGN WITH YOUR SKILLS?

Once you've selected your launch criteria, you can begin to consider how they align with your skills. After all, if you have one criterion that says, "I want a job that pays very well," you need to have the skills for an industry where the salaries tend to be generous. High-paying jobs tend to be high-risk and high-stress as well.

Next, we'll take a look at exactly what you bring to the table so you can begin to evaluate the opportunities your skills and experience provide.

PART TWO

———

WHAT YOU BRING
TO THE TABLE

WHAT DO YOU HAVE TO WORK WITH?

We had the opportunity to teach a sales class at University de Valle in Guatemala City to MBA students, and while we were there, Codie also did some individual coaching sessions. One of the students we met with was Javier, and during the course of our conversation, he mentioned that he doesn't like conflict and tries to avoid it. By nature, he always seeks consensus.

He wound up in a career where he spent a lot of time negotiating contracts for a local company with a large multinational discount retailer, and he was miserable. When it comes to negotiating contracts, this large retailer is a powerhouse. They know how to get their costs down, how to get fast delivery, and how to get good credit terms.

All day long, Javier was dealing with an aggressive negotiator who wasn't particularly interested in coming to a consensus, and he hated it. It wasn't until he met with Codie and completed a Gallup CliftonStrengths test that he realized his number one strength is harmony. Suddenly, his unhappiness on the job made sense, and he realized he needed to find another position that would play to his strengths.

Now, he works in a position managing people, and he spends most of his time helping them learn, grow, and develop their professional skills. He is thriving on the job, and he's happy because he is using his skills and working in an area that allows him to use his strengths.

Javier is perfect example of the importance of knowing your own strengths and finding a career that aligns with them. You need a good understanding of what you have to offer so you can analyze career opportunities and pursue the right ones. That way, if you come across a job description that doesn't match with your skills and strengths, you can walk away.

UNDERSTANDING YOUR OWN VALUE

In this chapter, we will help you recognize and articulate your skills and strengths so you can express them on a job application, résumé, or in an interview. We encourage you to begin creating a written inventory of them, something you can refine as you learn more about yourself.

You possess both *hard skills* and *soft skills*, which are defined as follows:

- Hard skills: Specific, tangible abilities that can be measured and defined, such as math, writing, and programming
- Soft skills: Less tangible traits, such as being a good conversationalist, a good listener, or a motivational team leader

When a professional tennis player wins a match, she is using her training and abilities to get the ball past her opponent. That's a hard skill. After the match is over, when she approaches the net, shakes her opponent's hand, and engages in a friendly conversation, that's a soft skill. If you want to fully utilize everything you have to offer on your team and in your organization, you need a perfect marriage of the two, but to be able sell yourself during a job interview, you have to know what they are and be able to communicate them effectively.

Too often, college students are encouraged to be well rounded: learn a little bit of everything. There's a danger in trying to be well rounded rather than focusing on your strengths, in that you gradually become decent at many things but not great at anything—a mile wide and an inch deep.

Mark Jones, CEO of Goosehead Insurance, the fastest-growing insurance company in the United States, says, "Bologna is well rounded. I prefer lopsided people who use their strengths and aren't focused on improving their weaknesses." He first said this in a class we were teaching, and it was a revelation. Companies want you to be really good at the specific skills that contribute to their business.

If you're well rounded, you're a jack of all trades and master of none. Dr. Litzenberg isn't very good at accounting. If he wanted to, he could take a number of accounting courses and spend countless hours trying to get better at it, but in terms of career success, he's better off spending those hours focusing on the things that will help him excel on the job. You possess skills and talents in a combination that makes you unique, so why not focus on those areas of uniqueness instead of trying to be something you're not? It will make you more engaged at work and give you an overall higher quality of life.

If you're in your early to midtwenties, you might not yet have a good sense of how your skills, preferences, and personality all fit together. You might not know what you really bring to the table, so you might struggle to communicate what you do well. As you consider your own skills and abilities, reflect on the following questions. By the time you begin evaluating job offers, you want to be able to articulate your answers to each of them. We recommend writing down your answers.

WHAT CAN YOU DO NATURALLY?

It's difficult to recognize your own natural abilities because they come as easy as breathing. They are simply things you do well whether you realize it or not. For example, you might naturally be a good public speaker. You might naturally be good at analyzing data, taking apart and putting together machines, or getting a group of people pumped up with your natural enthusiasm. One thing to note is that some of the things that come easily to you are areas of weakness for other people.

WHEN DO YOU FEEL SUCCESSFUL?

When was the last time you completed a task and felt energized and excited because you were in your element? Maybe you walked away feeling like you could conquer the world. We want you to think about a situation that causes this feeling of accomplishment so you can continue to put yourself in similar situations.

Push yourself even further in this direction so you will continue to grow and develop your skills in an area that excites you. Don't be afraid to go outside of your comfort zone. Comfort is easy, but it doesn't encourage growth.

WHAT ARE YOU DRAWN TO?

Never ignore the things that appeal to you because they might indicate areas where you would flourish in your career. For example, if you love to read multiple books at the same time, you might enjoy dealing with large amounts of information or data. If you're the kind of person at a party who loves to engage people in conversation, you probably excel at networking.

Think about the activities you are drawn to, the things you enjoy doing. Recognizing patterns of behavior in your life can help you identify them. By recognizing the things you're drawn to, you can find the ways they relate to your natural skills.

WHAT DO PEOPLE SAY YOU'RE GOOD AT?

Are there compliments that you regularly receive from friends, professors, or coworkers (that you probably tend to ignore)? Do people tell you that you're good at solving problems or analyzing data? Do they come to you for help when making a schedule? Are you able to plan for the future, setting five-, ten-, or fifteen-year goals?

Though it's good to be humble, it's helpful to have some idea of what skills and abilities other people notice in you. The compliments you receive provide valuable evidence for your natural strengths. Look to past successes to find those moments when you were recognized for excelling at particular tasks.

THE POWER OF PERSONAL ASSESSMENTS

One of the advantages of our technologically driven age is that you have access to a wide variety of online assessments that help you identify your strengths, why you think the way you do, and how you communicate. In particular, we recommend taking the Gallup: CliftonStrengths test (formerly StrengthsFinder), 5 Voices, and Myers-Briggs, all of which can be found online through a simple Google search.

GALLUP: CLIFTONSTRENGTHS

Gallup: CliftonStrengths is an online talent assessment that helps you discover what you naturally do best, learn how to develop your greatest talents, and use your customized results to live your best life. It measures your natural patterns of thinking, feeling, and behaving so you can discover your strengths. In the end, you receive a customized report, giving personalized insight on the top five of thirty-four distinct themes and how they appear in your life.

This is one of the most hyperindividualized assessments you can take—the chances that you and another person will have the same top-five strengths in the same exact order are one in thirty-three million—so we recommend it to our students and incorporate it into our program. More than twenty million people have taken the assessment.

Gallup: CliftonStrengths encourages you to focus on areas of strengths rather than areas of weakness, driven by the idea that your best bet for success lies in building on who you already are rather than trying to become someone you're not. As we said earlier in the book, despite what you might have been told in childhood, you can't be anything you want to be, but you can excel at what you already are.

Employers are impressed by self-awareness, so using Gallup: CliftonStrengths in response to the request, "Tell me about yourself," is bound to make a big impact in an interview. This kind of answer will certainly be more impressive than describing where and how you grew up.

Consider the example of our former student, Walker, who has an innate ability to effortlessly adjust to the shifting challenges he faces throughout the day. He appreciates not being bound to a strict timeline or action plan because it allows him to take advantage of opportunities the moment they arise. In our experience, Walker excels at coming up with strategic options, finding innovative solutions, and completing tasks that he is passionate about.

In his CliftonStrengths assessment, *Adaptability* was very high on his list, while *Discipline* was very low. Asking Walker to work in an environment with a monotonous routine and structure would drive him crazy, and he would be operating in an area where he was unable to use his strengths. While Walker could work at incorporating more routine into his life, it would have to be flexible in order for him to thrive.

Taylor, on the other hand, has *Discipline* as her number one strength, so she thrives on structure and routine. A few years ago, Taylor set out to accomplish a goal of losing weight through diet and exercise. She created a workout routine that fit her schedule, and she stuck with it every day no matter how hard or unbearable it was. By utilizing her *Discipline* strength, she was able to lose over a hundred pounds, and she continues to make healthy strides in her life. She has told us that without a daily regimen, she would not have been able to accomplish her goal so quickly.

These are two examples of people understanding and utilizing their strengths. We encourage you to take the assessment to see your own results. Keep in mind that the paragraph you read in your CliftonStrengths results will be different even from others who share the same top strength.

MYERS-BRIGGS TYPE INDICATOR

The Myers-Briggs Type Indicator is a personality inventory that uses the psychological types described by Carl Jung to provide you with insight on how you perceive the world around you and make decisions. In the end, you are assigned one of sixteen possible psychological "types," represented as a four-letter abbreviation, with each of the letters representing some aspect of the way you perceive and interact with the world around you. For example, if you're an INFP, the letters stand for *introversion, intuition, feeling,* and *perception.*

We would add one note of caution about Myers-Briggs. Just because you are identified as an introvert doesn't mean you won't thrive at a job that requires you to interact with the public. This is a common misunderstanding. We know a woman who is a highly successful salesperson for a French company in the United States despite being an introvert.

Because she is aware of her own introversion, she is able to work around this weakness by creating some personal motivation. She plays a game with herself in which she lines up paper clips on the left side of her desk, and every time she completes a sales call, she moves one paper clip to the right side of her desk. She doesn't allow herself to have a cup of coffee until she has moved ten paperclips. In this way, she is able to motivate herself, and when it comes to the actual sales presentation, that helps her to do quite well.

THE 5 VOICES

The 5 Voices is based on the idea that every individual has a natural leadership voice (the nurturer, the creative, the guardian, the connector, the pioneer) that can be leveraged for effectively leading teams. By learning what your leadership voice is, you can communicate more effectively, even if you're not in a leadership position. It helps ensure that people won't get offended or take what you say the wrong way, and it also teaches you to listen better and make quicker, more effective decisions.

OWN YOUR RESULTS

Gallup: CliftonStrengths, Myers-Briggs Type Indicator, and the 5 Voices are the three assessments we recommend most, but there are others. All of them can contribute to a deeper understanding of your own strengths and weaknesses, giving you a clearer sense of what you bring to the table.

When you get results from these tests, share them with

close friends and family. Their feedback on your results can provide deeper self-awareness, which will help you grow in your emotional intelligence. At the same time, the people who know you well can identify whether or not you've skewed the results of your assessments by introducing bias in your answers. In that sense, they can keep you honest.

Your goal is to *own* your results. These tests will reveal both strengths and weaknesses, and our human tendency is to obsess over the weaknesses. We're all flawed human beings. Shedding light on those flaws can be uncomfortable at first, but as you learn more about yourself, you need to appreciate your unique perspective, personality, and gifts. You don't have to succeed at everything, and it's okay to be *bad* at some things. Ultimately, you bring value to the table by having a unique set of thoughts, feelings, and strengths, and when you know what those things are, you can make the most of them in your career success.

The researchers behind these assessments have spent years developing them, investing countless hours to refine and improve the results they give. While these test results shouldn't be used *alone* to tell you the exact industry or company you should go into, they can help you identify a compatible environment. Ultimately, the more you understand yourself, the more you can recognize and articulate what you want in your relationships, life, and career.

We recommend sharing this information with your eventual boss because the results can also help them communicate more effectively with you. This is why so many companies are beginning to use them in their onboarding process. We also recommend including these strengths and indicators of your personality on your résumé and even on your business cards.

At this point, you should have a written inventory of your skills, strengths, and abilities, along with an awareness of your own personality and even weaknesses. This information will play a vital role in evaluating industries, companies, and opportunities for your career launch.

8

YOUR RÉSUMÉ

This might sound like a no-brainer, but we've had students come to us the evening before a job interview and say, "I guess I should get my résumé together. Can you help me?" It takes time to make a résumé look nice, so don't throw it together at the last minute. It should be nicely formatted, well written, up to date, and easy to read. If you rush it, you are more likely to make mistakes, and there's nothing more unprofessional than a résumé full of typos, poorly worded sentences, and wrong information.

Your résumé is an ongoing record of your accomplishments, so make it a living document. When you have a job interview, if your résumé is up to date, you can go back through it and tweak some of the information to make it more relevant to the job description.

YOUR RÉSUMÉ DOESN'T HAVE TO LOOK LIKE ANYONE ELSE'S

The standard résumé contains the following information:

- Name
- Address
- Career Objective Statement
- Education
- Work Experience
- Leadership/Volunteer Experience
- Skills
- Awards
- Professional References

All of this information is essential, but we believe that if you can differentiate yourself through your résumé, you will create an advantage going into a job interview.

We've watched HR recruiters at job fairs going through stacks of résumés. They scan them quickly and either keep or discard each one based on what does or doesn't grab their attention. You have a few seconds to catch their eye and stand out to survive the purge. There must be something in your résumé that makes them want to look deeper at you for the job.

For example, we had a student whose dream was to work at Ben & Jerry's. She had learned all about the company culture and knew that she would thrive there. To get the attention of recruiters, she printed her résumé on paper the color of pink bubble gum. In most companies, this would have been incredibly off-putting and might have killed her chances, but she knew Ben & Jerry's recruiters would appreciate it.

It worked. Her résumé caught their attention, and she was offered a job interview. This led to a job offer in the exact position she'd been hoping for, and she wound up getting the job. Company leaders told her they appreciated the combination of her experience and obvious creativity.

THE SCALE AND SCOPE OF YOUR ACCOMPLISHMENTS

Recruiters need to know about your accomplishments. If you're still in college, you might have some part-time work experience or an internship. Include it all. We know there are some majors where having a part-time job simply isn't possible, so if you didn't work during college, be sure to convey how you scheduled and spent your time. Ideally, you can show some not-for-profit activity or at least some campus organization activity.

You want to show the company's selection committee that you are capable and have a demonstrable work ethic. It's not easy to convey your work ethic in a résumé, and we recommend avoiding words like "capable," "good work ethic," or "honest." You can convey these qualities in other ways. For example, if you write, "I oversaw register transactions averaging two thousand dollars a day," it conveys honesty without using the word.

Focus on describing the work you've done. Don't be vague. Don't write sentences like, "I worked hard stocking the shelves." Instead, be specific about the work: "I supervised inventory practices by categorizing thirty food product lines." If you trained people, mention how many people you trained and how you trained them. Shed light on *specific* accomplishments. This applies equally to Relaunchers. If you grew sales by twenty percent, expanded a product line, or grew social media followers by a certain amount, let recruiters know.

INCLUDE POWERFUL KEYWORDS

Technology has made it easier than ever to submit an online application for a job, so company recruiters tend to get inundated, and many of these résumés come from people who are clearly unqualified but decide to "give it a shot" anyway. To deal with this increased volume in résumés, companies are using applicant tracking systems (ATS) to scan résumés for specific keywords the employer has selected. ATS software enables recruiters to sift through and sort hundreds of résumés at a time, quickly isolating any that are worth a closer look.

By anticipating the words that recruiters might look for, you give your résumé a greater chance of standing out. Of course, no company is going to provide a list of their preferred keywords, but a bit of research about the company and job position can provide some clues. Study the job description for distinct language that you can incorporate into the scale and scope of your accomplishments. Match keywords exactly. ATS software doesn't always recognize variations such as plurals, different verb tenses, or abbreviations.

Although this might seem like a strange game, it is a game you have to play. It's unfortunate that this shortcut almost certainly means some highly qualified candidates get overlooked by recruiters, but it's a reality everyone entering the job market must deal with due the increased volume of applicants.

NEVER EMBELLISH YOUR WORK HISTORY

It might be tempting to do so, but *never* fabricate, exaggerate, or embellish your past accomplishment or on-the-job responsibilities. It's a gamble some make, but getting caught could spell career suicide. You can finesse the wording, but always stay within the boundaries of truth.

If you were a teaching assistant for a class, don't state that you taught the course. Don't claim to have managed a veterinary clinic if you were cleaning out the kennels. People within industries talk, and word has a way of getting around. Sooner or later, fabricated claims get uncovered, and if you have a reputation for lying on your résumé, doors will start slamming in your face.

We heard about a young man who got hired after claiming on his résumé that he'd earned an MBA. Once he started working for the company, leaders noticed that anytime someone mentioned his MBA, he angrily deflected the conversation to something else. Eventually, they confronted him about this and learned that he'd lied. He didn't have an MBA. As a result, he lost the job and ruined his reputation in the industry.

It's not worth the risk! Don't do it.

WHERE ARE YOUR REFERENCES?

Either during the application process, on your résumé, or during your interview, you will need to provide some professional references. These are people who can vouch for your character, skills, and work ethic. You will draw these references from your professional network, which we'll talk about in Chapter Eleven.

For now, let us offer this warning, too; we find that students will list people as references without telling them. In some cases, they list people they haven't spoken to in years or haven't even met. When the company contacts the reference, the individual is blindsided. This has actually happened to us on a few occasions.

On one occasion, a student listed Codie as a reference without giving her a heads-up, so on a particularly early Saturday morning, a recruiter called to discuss the recruit. Codie woke up to this conversation unprepared to speak about the student, foggy from coming out of a deep sleep, and she hung up the phone knowing it could have been executed better.

When a company calls one of your references and gets a confused response, it damages your credibility. We will help you develop a healthy network that you can draw from in Chapter Eleven, but always warn people before you put them down as a reference or when you're about to send an application. Letting your references know when they should expect a call is the polite thing to do.

PREPARE TWO RÉSUMÉS

Everything we've just discussed should be incorporated into your *current* résumé, but we also believe it's a good idea to create a *future* résumé. To help you dream big about your career plans, your future résumé will be based on where you hope to be and what you hope to accomplish in the years ahead. Consider it a version of a company's vision board.

When Dr. Litzenberg was approaching his fortieth birthday, he realized he didn't have any international experience to show on his résumé, so he created an empty box at the end of his résumé and titled it *International Experience*. He then set out to create experiences to fill the box, volunteering to manage a study-abroad trip to France, as well as teaching courses in Guatemala, Australia, and Indonesia.

He also wanted to gain some experience in educational program review, so he created another empty box for it on his résumé. Then he arranged to participate on educational review teams at fourteen different American universities, as well as international program review teams in Australia, Armenia, and Canada. For this effort, he was given an award by the Association of Public and Land-grant Universities, but more importantly, he was able to fill the empty boxes on his résumé.

Codie wanted to acquire international experience as well, so she volunteered to teach a course in Guatemala, and she led a group of students on a study-abroad course across the United Kingdom. She also wanted to get some public speaking experience, so she actively sought out student organizations and community events for guest-speaking opportunities. As a result, her public speaking capabilities drastically improved, and she has been a keynote speaker for several large corporate and organizational banquets. In the future, she plans to expand this venture even more.

We recommend doing something similar with your future résumé. Add those areas of experience that you hope to acquire in the years ahead. Then begin working to fill the empty boxes. Wherever you are in the career launch, there are ways to acquire relevant experience now. For example, you can join student organizations or industry associations. If you want leadership experience, run for office in a student organization. Of course, you'll probably have to be involved in the organization for a while before you can run for office. If you want experience with public speaking, join an organization like Toastmasters.

Your friend Google can help you find relevant associations or organizations for just about anything you're interested in, and these groups make excellent additions to a résumé, though we recommend exercising a bit of caution and good judgment. Some clubs and organizations prey on people. They collect membership fees, promise networking opportunities, or access to resources but fail to keep those promises. Do research on any organization before joining. What do their constitution or mission statements say, and how well do you align with them? What do current *and* former members say about them?

Remember, organizations aren't simply for fun. You can develop several types of experience that will positively impact your career, including gaining leadership skills, refining your public speaking abilities, gaining experience with accounting or budgeting, and much more.

YOUR CORE COMPETENCIES

Once your résumé is in great shape, you're ready to begin increasing the seven core competencies we mentioned in Chapter Three: *mentoring, interviewing, networking, job shadowing, professionalism, travel,* and *reading.* We will explore each of them deeply so you are thoroughly prepared for your career launch.

Don't forget to revisit the career competencies chart from Chapter Three as you move through the following chapters. You should see your scores rise as you implement the tasks and exercises we provide.

PART THREE

———

YOUR CORE COMPETENCIES

9

MENTORS: THE RUDDER FOR YOUR CAREER LAUNCH

When Grant shared with us his frustrations about working at a large, successful software company and told us he'd been thinking about relaunching in the medical devices industry, our first question was, "Who is your mentor in the medical devices industry, and what do they think?"

"Uh, well," Grant replied with a shrug, "I don't have a mentor in that industry."

"Then who *are* your mentors?" we asked. "Who are the people that are helping you think through this big career decision?"

'Actually, I don't have *any* mentors."

No matter what industry you're considering, you *need* mentors, and we don't believe one mentor is enough. We strongly recommend creating a *mentor council* comprised of three to five industry people with relevant experience who can help you navigate the career path ahead.

We had a student who was interested in working in the chicken processing industry—until she did a summer internship at a local plant. No one had prepared her for the job, and two weeks before the end of her internship, she quit. She said, "I just couldn't look another eviscerated chicken in the face."

In retrospect, she should have had a mentor who worked in the industry. Then she could have asked about the job and gained a clearer sense of what it would be like before she entered into a doomed internship. Either the mentor could have helped her mentally prepare for the stomach-churning conditions, or she would have figured out it was the wrong industry for her through their conversations.

DO YOUR PART—FIND MENTORS

When Grant told us he didn't have any mentors, we didn't criticize him. Instead, we said something that we often tell Launchers: "You have to do your part." You have to find mentors and create a mentor council. After all, they're not going to find you.

At this point in your career plan preparations, we encourage you to think about who you want for mentors. Seek out thought leaders in your desired industry and tactfully establish relationships with them. They will become trusted confidants who can expose you to opportunities that you would more than likely not experience otherwise.

It's a common mistake for students to assume their professors, guidance counselors, advisors, or even parents can be the mentors for their career launch. While all of these people can provide help and motivation in various ways, they can't provide the real-world, practical advice you need for launching your career in a particular industry. We find that many Launchers have professors who are important to them, and that's great. However, while they may be great mentors for your course work, they are likely not the right people to guide you into the next stage of your career.

Your parents love you and they want to see you be successful and happy, but they probably aren't experts in your desired industry, and their mindset about launching a career was formed twenty-five years ago in a completely different cultural context. They simply can't give you the information you need to launch your career in today's environment and in your chosen industry. For that, you need a mentor council comprised of *at least three*, at most five, individuals with a variety of relevant skills, knowledge, and experience.

We always encourage students to do their due diligence in selecting mentors and not simply go with the first person who seems to know something about their industry. For example, we will have students come up to us sometimes and say, "Wow, the special speaker we had in class today was pretty good. Maybe I'll use him for my mentor. He works in my industry."

Just because someone works in the same space a student is interested in doesn't mean they're the right mentor. You need someone who has the *specific* experience and expertise to help you in the next stage of your journey. If you're a twenty-one-year-old student who's still in college, the sixty-year-old CEO of a large organization might not remember what it was like to be at your stage of a career launch, so they will struggle to speak to your specific needs if you're very early in your career.

One of our Launchers, Jacob, went to work as a sales representative in the citrus industry. He has a mentor with experience in the industry that he calls all the time. Any time Jacob has a question or concern about his job or industry, he says, "I'd better talk to my mentor about that."

This has been especially helpful to him because of the quirky nature of the citrus industry's annual schedule. Starting in the middle of November, everything becomes hectic because the fruit is ripe and has to be picked and shipped as soon as possible. As they say in the industry, "Sell it or smell it." You have to move fast. You can't hold on to the fruit, so you'd better know who to call to get things moving. In those frantic moments, when Jacob is stressed out and trying to make quick decisions, he's not alone. He can turn to his mentor for help, and it has gotten him through a few rough seasons.

So, where can you find these mentors? Your best bet is to utilize the amazing technology that is available to us today. LinkedIn is a powerful tool for reaching out and finding mentors, and it will play a vital role when we talk about networking as well. Just reach out to people, ask them to lunch, and establish a connection for an ongoing relationship. Don't let a fear of rejection prevent you from messaging someone directly, even if you've never met them in person.

That first message can be a little scary but, trust us, it happens all the time in most industries. The message can be as simple as, "Hey, I'd love to pick your brain sometime about the industry. Would you have some time to spare?" Showing interest in a field they are working in increases your likelihood of developing a relationship.

There are also professional associations for most industries that will have a list of members you can contact. Often, associations will have "happy hour" events or other social gatherings on university campuses, as well as conferences or meetings you can attend. These are great opportunities to mingle with potential mentors. Don't be afraid to ask in person if they're willing to meet. It's not unusual to ask, so they won't be shocked.

WORKING WITH MENTORS

Our trusted friend and colleague Lorenzo Gomez wrote a book called *The Cilantro Diaries* in which he talks about the importance of having your own personal board of mentors comprised of individuals you have personally selected and invited. In particular, we love Lorenzo's advice about having a wide variety of mentors from different backgrounds. These should be people who aren't afraid to tell you the truth, even if it's hard for you to hear.

Mentors fills in the gaps in your current skillset, experience, and knowledge base. If you only seek advice from people who are the same as you, they won't challenge you to think bigger or see a different perspective. You also need people who have experience in areas where you're weakest or least knowledgeable.

As the old proverb says, "If you want to go *fast*, go alone. If you want to go *far*, go together."

THE RECIPE FOR A MENTOR COUNCIL

Generally speaking, we recommend a mentor council comprised of at least *two* mentors who are in positions similar to the one you are pursuing or starting, *one* mentor who is a rung above your level, *one* mentor who holds the position you would like to have in five years, and *one* mentor who is entirely outside of your industry. This gives you a broad range of expertise to draw from because no single person will possess all of the knowledge you need at any particular stage in your career.

Create a list—a *mentor council directory*—of present, past, and potential future mentors, and make sure the contact information is correct and current (and easy to find). Once you have selected a mentor, it's important to cultivate your relationship with them. Always be authentic. Prove that you are who you say you are so you are always building trust. Don't try to impress a mentor with exaggerated stories about past accomplishments. Nobody likes a show-off. Don't present yourself in a dishonest way.

Communicate your goals so your mentor can begin to think of ways to help you achieve them. In addition, any time you meet with a mentor, come prepared with specific questions you want to ask. Be like a sponge, ready to soak up all the knowledge you can. Take notes that demonstrate to your mentor that you are invested and engaged in the conversation and make sure they know where your specific areas of need lie.

Learn to take feedback well. Remember, you are there to learn and grow, to have your perspective and understanding challenged, so grow a thick skin. Otherwise, you will shy away from asking your mentors how you can improve.

STEPS FOR MEETING WITH A MENTOR

First, always respect a mentor's time. If your mentor is someone of note in your chosen industry, then they are sure to be busy. If they aren't busy, then you probably don't want their advice. When planning a meeting, ask them how much time they have available and keep track of the time during your meeting. You might even use the timer on your smartphone to make sure you don't go over. Plan to meet with different members of your mentor council about once a month. Although you might communicate far more often than that, those in-person meetings make the biggest demands on their time, so keep them reasonable.

Second, always prepare at least three questions in advance, but don't read them off the page like a court reporter. You're supposed to be having a conversation. Make good use of your mentors. Ask for their advice about topics related to your career launch. For more help developing questions for your mentor meetings, you might check out the final pages of Tim Ferriss's book *Tribe of Mentors*, which provides an extensive index of questions and references to answers. Bear in mind, however, this is not an *exhaustive* list of mentor questions. You might also think about the emotional triggers that have caused you to select specific topics and questions. These can become a vital part of your mentor conversation as well.

Maintain a list of possible topics you can discuss with mentors. You can use this list as a reference when creating questions for an upcoming meeting. We recommend a meeting agenda that looks something like this:

- Discuss topics from the last sessions. Is there any follow-up?
- Introduce today's topics—at least three questions you've prepared.
- Select a time and place for the next meeting and confirm who will initiate contact (even if this is a regularly scheduled monthly meeting).

Be prepared to have crucial conversations—to be pulled out of your comfort zone. You may want to read the book *Crucial Conversations* to help you prepare for mentor meetings. Your mentors will have a lot of advice to offer, but it will be up to you to figure out how you're going to apply it. Remember, you get what you put in. This isn't a one-sided relationship, so always bring your best. If you come across a relevant article, share it with your mentors.

Additionally, always bring either a laptop or a notebook and pen to meetings. Don't wait to write things down until after you leave. You are five times more likely to remember what you write down.

FIRING A MENTOR

There are going to be times in your career when you need to fire a mentor because they are no longer helpful at this point in your career journey. Don't take this lightly. First, understand that it's *all right* to fire a mentor. Your needs evolve throughout your career, so it's good to have a mentor council that evolves along with you. To do that, you need to change the members of the council from time to time.

In the beginning, you need a mentor who can give advice about an entry-level position, but when you're in middle management, you need someone who can help you with middle management. You might even switch industries at some point in your career, making the expertise of some of your current mentors irrelevant.

Of course, when we recommend that you fire a mentor, we're not suggesting that you communicate it that way. Always thank the mentor and then say something like, "I appreciate what you've done for me. I'll keep in touch from time to time." You are moving them out of a mentor relationship, but you're keeping them in your network of contacts.

When you were in high school, you had mentors—maybe a teacher, a guidance counselor, a clergy member, or a coach—that gave you important advice about choosing the right college and major. You have since outgrown them because they can no longer provide the best advice for the next stage in your journey, but you will always be thankful for the time they spent with you. This will continue to be the case throughout your career, so be prepared to change mentors from time to time.

WHY WOULD SOMEONE WANT TO BE A MENTOR?

If you're like most Launchers, you might be wondering at this point why anyone of importance would want to spend time with you as a mentor. What do they get out of the relationship? Is it just some form of charity? Aren't they wasting their time?

Being a mentor is usually beneficial for mentors as well.

The time they spend with you provides a quick break from the regular stresses of their job, and it can be helpful for them to think through some of the topics and questions you bring to meetings.

You might be surprised at how soon in your career you will have the opportunity to pay it forward by becoming the next generation's mentor, but this will only happen if you're open to it and aware of the opportunities. To turn the question around, why should *you* want to be a mentor? Yes, it gives you a way of stepping away from the daily stresses of your job, but it also gives you a chance to keep up with the upcoming generation and to provide tangible advice to help someone advance in their career.

However, we believe the most important benefit of being a mentor is the way it makes you feel. When you are in tune with the needs and concerns of the people you manage, it makes you more sympathetic, and therefore more effective, at your job. Also, in a sense, it *is* charity or, more accurately, *philanthropy*. We are big believers in giving to others and making a difference. If you build up the people around you, your success will grow as theirs does.

DELIVERABLES TO SELF

1. Create a document or spreadsheet called "Mentor

Council" and save it to your desktop. It should contain a list of your past, present, and at least five potential future mentors that you haven't yet approached. It should also contain their contact information, but never text or call a mentor unless they have given you permission to do so. It is better to use email initially. As you build trust, you can ask for permission to use other means of communication. If you have access to your computer right now, pause a moment in reading this book and create your Mentor Council file.

2. Create a second document to record every meeting you have with your mentors. Include the time and date, along with any advice, encouragement, or constructive criticism they give you. This is a place to gather all of the notes you've taken during meetings. If you promised to follow up on something they said, record it and also add it to a to-do list on your calendar. It's not enough to tell someone you will get back to them. The mentor relationship is too important.

DAILY THINKING

Find a quiet moment during the day—even if it's only five minutes—to think about a question or topic you can add to your list for an upcoming mentor meeting. You might be going about your business and suddenly think, "I should ask my mentor how I can approach an immediate supervisor to ask for a promotion." Pull out your smartphone or tablet or sit down at your computer and immediately add this question to your list.

Always be on the lookout for topics you can discuss with your mentor and be prepared to jot them down and add them to your list. Also, always be on the lookout for potential new mentors for your future mentor councils.

RECOMMENDED READING

The Cilantro Diaries: Business Lessons from the Most Unlikely Places by Lorenzo Gomez

Tribe of Mentors: Short Life Advice from the Best in the World by Timothy Feriss

Crucial Conversations: Tools for Talking when Stakes Are High by Kerry Patterson, Joseph Grenny, Ron McMillan, and Al Switzler

THE INTERVIEW

The summer before she started graduate school, Codie interviewed for several summer internship opportunities. When she showed up to one of the interviews, she thought she was well prepared, having researched the department and internship program. Throughout the interview, she made sure to mention some of the information she had gleaned about the program.

About halfway through the interview, one of the interviewers mentioned the department he worked for, and Codie's blood went cold. She was in the wrong interview, and she'd been referencing a different department and internship program the whole time. There was no easy way out. She attempted to adjust and shift her answers to the correct program, but it was too late. She knew she wasn't going to get the internship.

Job interview mistakes are usually subtler than this, but they can shut the door to a great opportunity just as completely. If you don't get the interview right, it will kill your chances of landing the career position you want, and it doesn't take much to look like a fool. One blatant error, bad answer, weird moment, or inappropriate question can derail the whole thing, so always show up prepared with the right information and attitude, and make sure you reference the correct company in your interview!

Never just show up to an interview and try to fake it. You must have a plan, and you must have a clear sense of what you're getting into.

MASTERING THE JOB INTERVIEW

In this chapter, we will discuss the emotionally intelligent aspects of creating an effective résumé, differentiating yourself during a job interview, and being able to eloquently describe what you bring to the table. Remember the five Ps of interviewing: *Poor Preparation Produces Poor Performance!*

You are interviewing the company as much as they are interviewing you. Having this mindset can eliminate some of the stress. Have you ever walked into a job interview feeling incredibly nervous? Chances are you didn't do well, or the interviewers could tell. When you're a nervous wreck, you tend to stumble over your words and struggle to come up with quick, effective responses.

Nowhere is it more important to have appropriate emotional responses than during an interview. Your emotional triggers will be highly active since you will have an underlying worry about responding appropriately. This can make you almost paranoid about certain questions you are asked, as you wonder, "What are they really trying to get at? Is there a *correct* answer to this?"

There is almost a sense of interrogation during a job interview, and even the most seasoned professional might bristle at some of the questions. When they ask if you have relevant experience, that can trigger a whole host of emotional responses, depending on how you left your last job, or you may be obliged to respond, "I am just graduating and haven't had any experience." All of these emotional responses can be managed with appropriate emotional intelligence education.

Nothing feels worse than walking out of an interview that you know you just tanked. It makes you want to crawl under a rock. We want to get you past the anxiety so you can approach job interviews with confidence, knowing you are fully prepared and equipped to make a great impression. We will discuss some tips for being more confident in Chapter Sixteen when we deal with negative self-talk.

DIFFERENTIATE YOURSELF TO LAND THE INTERVIEW

Before you can dominate a job interview, you have to be *selected* for a job interview. Any decent job opportunity is going to have many people applying for it, especially if there's an online application process. Unless you distinguish yourself, you are simply another piece of paper in a stack of résumés.

We recommend sending your résumé overnight to the HR manager, VP of Sales, or VP of Marketing, depending on which department the job is in. Eric, a student in our sales program, loved the outdoors, and he really wanted to work for an outdoor brand like YETI or Mossy Oak. He applied online for an open sales position at YETI, but he knew he had to somehow stand out from the hundreds of other applicants who wanted it.

He knew YETI's slogan is "Wildly Stronger: Keeps Ice Longer," so he purchased a two-pound dumbbell and wrote the slogan, "Wildly Stronger: Keep Customers Longer." Then he downloaded his entire application, résumé, and cover letter and overnighted them to the VP of sales at YETI along with the dumbbell.

The next morning, he received a rejection letter. The position had already been filled. However, as he later learned, when the VP of Sales received his package, he walked over to the HR manager's desk, dropped the package in front of him, and said, "Even if we don't have an open position, we are interviewing this guy."

As it turned out, another position did open up. Eric got his interview, and he was offered the job. Now, he gets to work in an industry he is passionate about.

Another student of ours ordered a pizza and had it sent to the company she wanted to work for, but she gave the delivery driver some unusual instructions. When the pizza arrived, company leaders saw that a single slice had been removed, and a note had been written on the box that said, "I am the missing piece of your organization." Yes, it's *cheesy*, but it worked. She now works for the company. I'm sure you wouldn't *disa-brie* with how powerful something like that can be. The company told us they were pretty *fondue* of it.

PREPARE FOR THE INTERVIEW BEFOREHAND

Never approach an interview without researching the company first. Otherwise, you risk appearing unprepared, inadequate, and uninterested. We recommend spending at least three hours learning about their products

NEVER GHOST AN INTERVIEW OR JOB OFFER

We find that students will sometimes book five different interviews, get a job offer with the first one, and just not show up to the rest of the interviews—an unfortunate practice called ghosting. Even worse, sometimes they will get a job offer, accept it, but then say, "I told the company I'll take the job, but I'm going to look for a better offer in the meantime."

Employers have complained to us about applicants not showing up to scheduled interviews or not showing up for the first day on the job without even sending a text or email beforehand. We can't say this strongly enough. Never ghost a job interview. It burns bridges that might hinder future employment, and your rude behavior can negatively impact the reputation of your peers. A company that has a student from a particular university ghost an interview might be reluctant to interview other students from that same university.

In the professional world, this makes company leaders furious. When it happens with one of our students, those company leaders get mad at us. Most importantly, as a company leader pointed out to us, if you accept a job interview for a position you do not want, it closes the door to someone else who might have been successful in the role. If you fail to show up, you've wasted your own time, you've wasted company time, and you've potentially done harm to the career launch of another person. If you always say yes, it doesn't give someone else an opportunity to do so.

Sometimes, parents are complicit in this behavior, encouraging their child to accept a job offer and then continue searching for a better job offer. This is incredibly unprofessional. If you absolutely must back out of a prior commitment, contact the company, be honest about it, and apologize for the inconvenience. If you made a mistake in accepting an interview or job offer, own the mistake. Don't play victim to circumstances. Be respectful of the interviewer and their time and effort.

Bear in mind, this goes both ways. With the increased number of people interviewing for positions, HR managers sometimes don't follow through on the next steps of the interview process. We don't condone this behavior and understand the frustration it causes when it happens to you.

and services, primary competitors, and company culture. Glassdoor.com is a great website for acquiring much of this information.

Once you've studied the company, prepare specific questions about each of these areas that you can ask interviewers. This level of interest in the company will score you brownie points with recruiters. Remember, you want to show interest in the *specific* job opportunity and company you're interviewing for. A job interview is not simply a conversation about your skills and abilities, so always do your research beforehand.

We recommend practicing your job interview skills. A mentor can help you with this. They should be familiar with the kinds of questions you will encounter during a real job interview. As further refinement of your skills, film yourself during these practice interviews and review your own performance. This might feel uncomfortable at first. Most people don't enjoy watching themselves on video, but it's the perfect way to refine your approach.

DRESS THE PART

Dressing well is particularly important for your job interview. Whether or not it's fair, people form an opinion of you within the first thirty seconds of meeting you, and how you dress is a *huge* factor in that initial judgment.

If you show up to a job interview in wrinkled clothes or wear something that is stained, too revealing, or a fashion faux pas, it's going to damage your first impression and hurt your chances. You don't have to be a fashion guru to figure out what to wear. We recommend the following simple rule of thumb:

If you have any question about wearing it, you probably shouldn't.

There's no excuse for wearing wrinkled clothes. If you don't like ironing, you can buy a $20 steamer on Amazon. It will change your life. If you have a nice suit or dress, now is the time to pull it out of the closet and get it dry cleaned.

The clothes you wear do more than contribute to a good first impression. Research shows it also affects your mental and physical performance. If you feel good about what you're wearing, you will do better during the interview. Tailor your outfit to the industry. You don't want to be overdressed *or* underdressed. If it's a company where everyone wears a hard hat and steel-toed boots, you don't want to show up to the interview in an Armani suit. Don't be afraid to ask the HR manager about preferred attire. Specifically, ask if they prefer business casual or business professional.

BRING TANGIBLE EVIDENCE OF YOUR CAPABILITIES

Most candidates will bring a résumé to their job interview. The recruiter will almost certainly have a copy of the résumé with them already, but you may want to add specific experiences you have had since sending in the résumé. Bringing a copy with you to the interview allows you to point out specific experience that is most relevant.

We also recommend bringing samples of work you've completed in the past that is applicable to the job opportunity. This might take the form of charts and graphs showing how you increased sales volume or helped your company grow. It might take the form of a portfolio of artwork or articles you've written. Whatever you bring, be prepared to leave these things with the interviewer.

AVOID USING BLANKET STATEMENTS

It's common for interviewers to ask candidates, "What are your strengths and weaknesses?" This question is intended to test your self-awareness, and it's very common for people to answer by giving vague statements like, "I'm a team player. I'm good at multitasking. I don't procrastinate."

These kinds of vague statements make no impact at all, but candidates assume it's what recruiters want to hear.

Instead, we recommend diving deep into what you really bring to the table. Use information gleaned from self-assessment tests like CliftonStrengths to give a highly personalized answer. It might sound something like this:

"The value I bring to the table is that I enjoy analyzing large groups of data and communicating the overall structure. I'm also great at breaking down problems into digestible chunks."

When it comes to weaknesses, many candidates are terrified of giving an answer that will make them look bad, so they often fall back on the old standby, "My weakness is that I'm a perfectionist." Even if this is an honest answer, dig a little deeper. Maybe the truth is not that you're a perfectionist so much as you're afraid of failure.

The point is, you want to avoid giving interviewers the same blanket answers that they hear all the time. When you start feeding them these lines, they're going to mentally check out. They've heard it a million times.

INTERVIEW YOUR INTERVIEWERS

When you approach a job interview with the idea that you are also interviewing your interviewers, it removes some of the pressure you feel. Look at it as an opportunity to see if you are a great fit for the company. Ask questions that gauge the culture, work-life balance, or any other topic related to the job, company, or industry that you feel is important. Also, be sure to refer back to your career selection criteria to compare your metrics to their expectations for this position.

Always have questions prepared because at the end of most interviews, recruiters are going to give you an opportunity to ask. If you don't have any questions for them, they will take this as an indication of a lack of interest. If you're unsure of what to ask, we recommend the following questions.

- What sets you apart from your competitors?
- How do you create and sustain competitive advantage?
- How long have you been at this company, and what has kept you here this long?

You don't have to wait until the end of the interview to ask questions. You can tag them to the ends of your answers. Suppose a recruiter asks if you're a team player. You respond in the affirmative and give some evidence or a story to back up your answer, but you can then add a related question for the interviewer: "Is being a team player an important part of the company culture? How important is it with this particular job?"

With many jobs, you will participate in a *series* of interviews, and the first one might be merely a screening interview, which doesn't give you much opportunity to ask questions. However, as you progress through the interview series, you will find opportunities, even if you have to raise your hand and say, "I would like to ask a quick question, if that's okay." Though we recommend preparing these questions in advance, we don't recommend reading them off the page. When you ask, you want it to come across as a moment of genuine interest in the company.

People love talking about themselves, their jobs, and their companies, so if you can get your interviewers to open up, they will remember the interaction with you in a more positive light. At the same time, you are shedding more light on the company and culture, so you can make a more informed decision about accepting a possible job offer. People also like to hear their own names, so be sure to use the interviewer's name.

HAND THEM YOUR BUSINESS CARD

Even in this age of technology, it's still important to have a business card you can personally hand to people. When you go into the interview, hand them your card, and they will be more likely to remember you and know your name. It's an age-old trick that is as effective as ever.

You can get a box of business cards at Vistaprint or similar online companies for around twenty dollars. Your card doesn't need to include much more than your name and contact information—chiefly your cell phone number and email address—at this point. If you want, you can also include your major, and we've seen some Launchers put their five strengths from their Gallup: CliftonStrengths results or their LinkedIn profile on the back.

It might sound like a simple thing, but a business card does differentiate you. We've been in career fairs where industry representatives had a stack of two hundred résumés, and the one that got placed on top of the stack had a business card stapled to it.

You can also ask the interviewer for their business card. If for some reason they don't have one, bring a piece of paper with you so you can write down their first and last name. Make sure you get the spelling correct. This is important because a day or so after the interview, you can either send them an email or message them on LinkedIn and say something like, "Hey, great interview. I appreciate it." Consider mentioning something that was said during the interview that resonated with you.

SEEK CLARIFICATION AND AGREEMENT TO YOUR ANSWERS

When you give an answer to the interviewer, particularly when speaking about your own skills, abilities, or experiences, it's a good idea to say something like, "Do you see how that would benefit your company? Would you say it's a good fit for your culture?" You might even go so far as to say, "Do you believe I answered that question in a way that would help your company be successful?"

The idea here is to seek clarification as you go through the interview process. Many interviewers today approach their job almost clinically. They're looking for key information and filling out forms, so you force their hand by getting them to step back and analyze your performance. It also gives you an idea of how well you're doing so you don't have to wonder and worry.

CLOSE THE INTERVIEW WELL

If you believe a job opportunity is right for you, end the interview by asking for the job. There is no stronger indication to a recruiter that you have a genuine interest. First, summarize the most important points that you've covered, especially those that resonated with your interviewer, reminding them of what you bring to the table, then close by saying something like, "Is there anything that would indicate I'm not a suitable candidate for this position?" When they say no, you are helping them make that final unconscious check mark that tells them you're a solid candidate for the job.

You can even be so bold as to say, "I could see myself working well with this company. May I have the job?"

We had a student named Cole who interviewed for a position at Mustang Cat, a global equipment company. Out of hundreds of people who applied for the position, he was the only one who explicitly asked for the job at the end of the interview. It made him something of a celebrity at the company. When he showed up for his first day, everyone had already heard about him. During his second week on the job, he was visiting a worksite when another employee said, "Hey, aren't you the famous guy who asked for the job?" That simple act of boldness not only won over the recruiter but established his reputation at the company.

You're not trying to put the interviewer on the spot. If they respond, "We'll let you know," accept that answer and don't badger them. Asking for the job shows that you're interested and passionate about the job. We've seen it work many times.

NO ONE IS AN ISLAND

Now that you know how to give a great interview, you can begin building a professional network to help you thrive in your career. No one is an island, and you're not going into this all by yourself. There are plenty of people out there who can support and encourage you along the way.

Next, we will show you how to build your professional network.

11

NETWORKING

Just the other day, a student approached us and said, "I'm looking for a job in the pharmaceutical industry. Do you happen to know anyone in the industry I could talk to?" As it happened, we knew some industry reps from pharmaceutical companies, so we made a connection. In the end, it led to the student getting a job in her chosen profession.

In our office, we maintain an entire library of books containing contact information for people in various industries that we've connected with over the years. Students come to us all the time looking to network with people in their chosen industry. Thanks to our connections, we also stay current on internship opportunities, which we display on a monitor in front of our office.

As you approach your career launch, it is important to begin building and utilizing a professional network. You can't do it all by yourself—you need connections. In fact, we require the students in our program to add at least three industry people to their network by the end of each semester.

The people in your network can provide you with career opportunities and share valuable industry information that will keep you up to date on news and trends. Rather than simply scrolling through pages of job listings on one of the many employment search engines, you can turn to your network to find out about the opportunities that are a great fit for you. They can also provide the advice you need to gain an advantage in landing those jobs.

Having a network also allows you to develop partnerships with people who have similar interests and who can contribute to your professional development. Some of the people in your network will make excellent references for your résumé. Maybe you'll find someone willing to invest in a business venture, loan you some money, or cosign a loan. You never know how your network might help you.

Also, never forget that it is important for you to give back to your network. In fact, the best way to maintain a responsive network is to offer help when they ask.

DEVELOPING YOUR NETWORK

There are plenty of ways to build and expand your network. We recommend joining industry associations and alumni groups because these kinds of organizations have regular activities where you can meet and mingle with other members. Be bold. Don't be afraid to ask people at these events to be in your network.

You can also network with people on social media platforms like LinkedIn and Facebook, though this is a little more difficult. We believe you have a better chance when you speak to people face-to-face, so get out there and shake hands. Move around in professional circles and get to know people. You can use social media to make the initial contact, but you need to move to a phone conversation or Skype fairly soon. Dan Schawbel wrote a book called *Back to Human* which speaks about the importance of making connections in creating a greater sense of fulfillment, productivity, and engagement, while preventing burnout and turnover.

If all of this sounds intimidating, bear in mind that industry professionals are used to networking. They're doing it themselves constantly, and more people are willing to join your network than you realize. Just ask. Your question can be as direct as, "Would you be in my network?"

A MENTOR COUNCIL VERSUS A NETWORK

Your network is comprised of a much broader range of people than your mentor council, and most of the relationships are fairly casual. Your mentors will be part of your network, but not everyone in your network will be a mentor.

With a mentor, you want to stay in regular contact, but many of the people in your network come and go. You might only see them at industry events or organizational meetings that you're both members of. We recommend maintaining occasional contact with everyone in your network so they know you still value the relationship, but there's no need to schedule regular meeting times with everyone. If you haven't spoken to someone in your network in three years, they probably no longer consider themselves part of your network.

Remember, just because someone is older and wiser and more influential than you are doesn't mean they need to be your mentor. Refer back to the chapter on mentors for specific qualities that a mentor should possess. Some influential people aren't mentor material for your specific career goals or your current stage in the journey, but they can still be a vital part of your broader network.

KEEPING IN TOUCH

How often should you keep in touch with the people in your network? We recommend making some kind of contact with every individual in your network at least four times a year—once a quarter. It doesn't have to be any more than a few sentences in an email, but keep in touch. Consider reaching out on social media when an important event occurs. The method of contact isn't important as long as you keep in touch.

Some of these people might wind up becoming references on your résumé, and you don't want a recruiter to contact them during the hiring process only for the reference to say, "I haven't talked to this person in years. I have no idea if they're any good for this particular job."

As we said in the previous chapter, always give someone a heads-up when you put them down as a reference. Make a friendly reconnection first. That way they will expect the call, which gives them time to think about what they want to say. You're trying to build authentic relationships here, not just use people for your own ends.

Remember, your mentors are the ones you call on frequently when you have a question or concern. Maintain a healthy balance with the other people in your network. Don't call them constantly with questions. The relationships you have within your broader network are more casual and friendly; they aren't everyday problem solvers.

YOU GET WHAT YOU PUT IN

The relationships in your network are give and take. You will get out of them what you put into them. If you view them as one-sided—as if your contacts are only there to serve your needs—people are likely to cut ties with you. No one wants to feel used or taken advantage of.

Try to give to them as much as they are giving to you. A gift or at least a card on their birthdays might not be a bad idea. Maybe you've read a good book you think they would enjoy. Send them a copy.

It's a good idea to send a gift along with any request. For example, when we ask someone to attend an event, we often send a book along with the invitation. However, this isn't a quid pro quo. You're not bribing people to do things for you. A gift shows that you want to give as much as you want to take. If someone in your network asks you to do something for them—maybe speak at an event or read an article they've written and provide feedback—be open to it.

A friendly greeting from time to time with no strings attached is often enough. Keep the conversation going so it's an actual relationship.

MAINTAIN YOUR CONTACT LIST

Create an Excel spreadsheet or Google doc or even a small database with all of your network contacts and keep it up to date. Categorize contacts by industry and company. Organizing your contact list is very important. A jumbled list of names with no sequence will be practically useless.

If you are keeping in regular contact with people, you will know when they change companies or job responsibilities or get new contact information. Update the information in your contact list as soon as possible so you don't forget.

DON'T MAKE A FOOL OUT OF YOURSELF

If you're invited to a happy hour event with people from your network, make sure to moderate your behavior. Don't get hammered and make a fool out of yourself. You don't want to do damage to your network relationships during those rare occasions when you're in the same room together.

By the same token, think carefully about how you dress when attending an event with people in your network. We strongly encourage you to dress conservatively. Avoid the short dress, the loud socks, or anything wild and crazy (unless it's a costume party).

A QUICK LIST OF NETWORK DOS AND DON'TS

- DO join or attend associations and organizations where you can meet potential network contacts.
- DO give as much as you get from your network.
- DO keep a contact list of people in your network.
- DO maintain your network contact list, constantly adding, removing, or updating contact information.
- DO stay in contact with each person in your network at least four times a year.
- DO use social media wisely.
- DON'T put someone as a reference if you haven't been in contact with them and warned them first.
- DON'T make a fool out of yourself at networking events.

RECOMMENDED READING

Back to Human: How Great Leaders Create Connection in the Age of Isolation by Dan Schawbel

JOB SHADOWING

We had a student named Katie who spent a day job shadowing John, a chemical salesperson who had more than twenty years of experience in his industry. John was impressed with the questions Katie asked, as well as her obvious interest in the industry. As he later said, she seemed inquisitive and emotionally mature. He also noted her experience on campus as a student recruiter for Texas A&M.

After a day of job shadowing, he offered Katie a summer internship, which turned out to be a very positive experience for her and the company. Upon her graduation, Katie launched her career with another company in the same industry, but she maintained contact with John.

She worked with the other company for two years, and

during that time, she realized her career interests and work style were a better fit for John's company. Since she had maintained contact with him, she was able to approach him and say, "I wish I was working for you instead. Your company culture is a better fit."

As it turned out, John's company had a great opening for Katie. She went to work for his company, and she has now enjoyed eight successful years there. This perfect opportunity was made possible because she job shadowed John years earlier.

THE VALUE OF JOB SHADOWING

Job shadowing not only provides the experience you need to choose between job opportunities based on your launch criteria, but it also gives you a chance to meet people who may become mentors. In some cases, you may even wind up working for them.

Job shadowing can also provide the clarification you need to avoid launching in the wrong industry or with the wrong company. Codie learned this from her own job shadowing experience in college. She thought she wanted to go into the oil and gas industry because it seemed exciting and a great place to make a lot of money.

She arranged a job shadowing opportunity with a national

oil company and spent the day riding around with a representative. She still vividly remembers visiting an oil derrick and seeing another employee who had been working on the equipment all day. He was completely covered in oil, but it didn't seem to bother him. Just another day at the office.

The workers stood there for long minutes talking about fittings and flanges and pipes, and Codie had a moment of stark clarity: "This just isn't for me." Now that she had experienced it for herself, it became clear that working in this part of the oil and gas industry didn't appeal to her at all.

Without that job shadowing experience, she would have maintained her romanticized view of the industry, and she would have pursued a job with an oil and gas company. It would have been a miserable experience, inevitably necessitating a difficult career relaunch at some point down the road.

That's the beauty of job shadowing. In one day, you get a good look at the culture and management structure, and you gain a sense of what the actual experience of working in the industry looks and feels like. There are certain realities of working at a particular company in a particular industry that aren't obvious until you spend time on the job.

If you have properly weighted your launch criteria, job shadowing gives you a chance to match what you're looking for with what you see on the job. Sometimes, students come back from job shadowing, and their expectations are validated. Other times, they have their eyes opened, and they are saved from making a poor career launch decision. For that reason, we strongly recommend job shadowing with at least a couple of different companies. You might just prevent yourself from making a terrible mistake.

Launchers often have romanticized notions about their chosen career field. Job shadowing can clear up those misconceptions. For example, maybe you've watched a few seasons of *CSI*, and now you think you want to become a forensic scientist. A day on the job with a real forensics team will clear up many of the ideas you picked up from the show. You might be shocked to learn how much time they spend doing unglamorous lab work.

Nothing provides the level of exposure that job shadowing does. In fact, it's the only way to truly discover what a job is like. We often have industry representatives speak to our classes and explain what they do, but this just isn't as effective for students as being in the work environment and seeing it for themselves.

Some students worry that they will be a burden. "I don't

want to bother anyone while they're at work," they'll say. However, job shadowing is a common practice, and it gives companies the opportunity to interact with the future workforce.

DON'T AIM TOO HIGH

Don't aim too high for your first time. A CEO will have some expertise to share, but their experiences on the job are much different than what you will experience when you launch your career. Remember, although the CEO may set the overall tone and culture for the firm, they don't generally do the hiring and may not be in tune with the entry-level job experience.

Ideally, it's better to follow someone who either has the job that you want or has done it in the past. For example, if you want to go into sales, it might be a good idea to job shadow with a vice president of sales. Not only would they have a clear understanding of the culture and industry, but they can speak to the entry-level work experience.

WHEN SHOULD I DO JOB SHADOWING?

Job shadowing is most productive when you're in college because it helps you formulate your career launch criteria and gain insight into an industry that has piqued your interest. It's a little trickier for Relaunchers. Once you've launched your career, it's going to be much more difficult to schedule a job shadow without alerting your current employer that you're dissatisfied with your job. That doesn't mean you shouldn't do it, but you have to be a lot more careful about how you approach it. Be very up front when job shadowing a company, especially if they are a competitor. Don't make it seem like you are trying to obtain competitive information from them.

Some students think of job shadowing as a homework assignment, and they complain that they don't have time for it. "I already have sixteen hours of class a week," they will say, "and on top of that, I work twenty hours a week."

If that's your current thinking, we recommend a shift in your mindset. Job shadowing isn't homework. It's more like a full-day job interview, and it's part of your career preparation. Make it a priority. You will be amazed what you can learn for a one-day investment of your time. A full-day experience is ideal, but half days are also an option.

FINDING A PROFESSIONAL TO FOLLOW

We've helped students create thousands of job shadowing experiences, so we've heard all the excuses. The most common excuse is, "I have no idea how to find someone to shadow." You might be having the same thought. If you've never done it before, the prospect can be intimidating.

Let us calm your fears. Most professionals think being shadowed on the job is a great idea. They like the idea of sharing their experiences and career successes. Many business leaders have told us they enjoy the opportunity to help young people with big dreams and lots of questions. However, the way you ask is important.

If you're already working part time or doing an internship at a firm, your own company is a good place to start. Identify someone in the company who has a job you would like to have and ask if you could follow them for a day. Be careful how you communicate this. You don't want to sound like you're gunning for their job. Format your questions so the focus is more on the industry and company than their specific job. Of course, we want you to think big, so take the time to search for other companies you can explore and shadow as well.

A second way to find someone to shadow is to ask your mentors if they know anyone in their industry who would be willing to let you spend a day on the job with them. Explain that you won't waste this professional's time or distract them at work, that you merely want to observe their daily routine. You may even consider shadowing one of your mentors, depending on their position in the firm and industry.

You can also find someone to shadow in industry associations and alumni groups. Don't be afraid to ask. No one's going to be offended that you think they're worth following around on the job. People are more willing than you probably realize, and asking is not that big of a deal. When you ask, tell them the reason you want to shadow them. For example, you could say, "You are a very successful marketing manager, and I am considering entering your industry. Could I shadow you for a half day?"

Remember, their time is their most valuable resource. When our students tell us the person they've asked to job shadow refused, the most typical reason given is, "I'm too busy." To allay that concern, we tell students to let their potential job shadow know up front that they won't take any of their time. You can add something like, "I won't take any of your time, I just want to follow someone as successful as you."

A final place you can find opportunities for job shadowing is through LinkedIn. Search for a company you're interested in, look through the list of people employed by the company, and message them on their LinkedIn profile. Codie made the connection that led to her job shadowing experience through LinkedIn.

By the way, job shadowing isn't simply for Launchers or Relaunchers. At all levels of your career, you can benefit from shadowing people on the job. We've even job shadowed several former students at different levels in their companies to keep fresh on what is going on in their respective industries.

ASKING A PROFESSIONAL THE RIGHT WAY

On the one hand, you have to show respect for a job shadow prospect, but on the other hand, you must be bold. You are more likely to win them over if you express interest in them, in their company, and in their industry.

They are also more likely to agree to it if you require very little effort on their part. Tell them, "I just want to watch what you do at work. You don't have to do anything special." If they're reluctant to bring you in to their workplace, see if they would be willing to meet you first to chat. We've had students take a job shadow prospect to breakfast or lunch to get acquainted with them. It's the best twenty dollars you will ever spend. As we continue to say, you've spent one hundred thousand dollars on your college education, don't be afraid to spend a few more dollars to help in a successful career launch. The professional will usually spring for the tab on their expense account, but be prepared to pay just in case they don't.

In our experience, ninety percent of job shadow prospects say yes as long as Launchers ask correctly. Always be respectful. We had a student call up someone they'd found on LinkedIn and, with no prior notice, ask, "Is it okay if I come over on Tuesday afternoon about two o'clock? I need to talk to you." He got turned down. It's pretty easy to say no to a rude approach like that.

The most important people in the industry will have gatekeepers standing between them and you. Before you can ask about a job shadow, you have to win the favor of the gatekeeper, which will typically be a secretary or office associate. Your best bet is to explain who you are and exactly what you'd like to do. We find it effective to say something like, "I'd like to learn a little bit from their experience." Express interest in the individual, their work, and their company, then ask, "How do I get on the schedule?" Provide some options for availability and reassure the gatekeeper that you have no intention of taking them away from their responsibilities. You just want to observe them on the job to get an idea of what their day looks like.

Most of the people you will want to job shadow are very busy, so make sure they know you're not going to get in the way. It's a good idea to have some questions to ask, but reserve them for the downtime between meetings or when they are walking somewhere, and limit it to thirty minutes out of the day. Prepare questions in advance so you can make efficient use of their time.

We recommend asking questions about the actual job experience and the company or industry culture. That's why you're there, after all. Align the questions with your launch criteria. Find out about the things that matter most to you. "How many nights a week do you work in this field? What's the expected work week like? Is there a good opportunity for advancement?" You might ask for advice about your résumé. "What kind of things on a résumé would impress the leaders in this company?"

Be respectful about the questions you ask. Some questions will seem rude. If you ask someone their salary, they will probably tell you, "None of your darn business." You can obtain the same information by asking differently. Make it less personal. "How much can someone earn in this position after eighteen years of experience?"

If their schedule is just too busy to fit you in, even for a short job shadow, they might at least recommend someone else. By the way, if someone turns you down, it's not the end of the world. This is another time when emotional intelligence is important. Make sure you don't overreact to rejection. They aren't saying no to you personally, they are saying no to the situation due to the circumstances.

FOLLOW UP AFTER A JOB SHADOW

Your follow-up to a job shadow is the most important part of the experience. You're learning from someone who has ten, twenty, or thirty years of experience in a job you would like to have, so make the most of it.

First, immediately after the job shadow, write them a personalized, handwritten letter to express your gratitude for the experience. Send this no more than three days afterward.

It could be as simple as a card that says, "Thanks for letting me tag along with you the other day. You helped me explore the inner workings of your company and culture, and I appreciate it." Include a business card. If you don't have any business cards yet, this is a good excuse to get some. If you ask questions about your résumé during the job shadow, you can also include your résumé with the note.

Second, you can follow up the informal thank-you letter with a professionally formatted letter within ten business days. You are thanking them again, but this time, you can mention the date of the job shadow and identify at least three takeaways or lessons you learned from the experience. Consider the wording of this letter very carefully because it may be shared with their supervisor or other company leaders. If you end up applying for a position at the company, this letter will serve as a powerful touch-point with leaders and could give you an edge during the interview process.

A Launcher named Shelby did a ride-along with someone from a food distribution company, and she was able to refer to this high-impact experience when she later interviewed for an internship with them. The fact that she already had familiarity with the company culture impressed her interviewer and helped her get the internship. This kind of experience shows genuine interest in a company and makes you stand out.

More significantly, Shelby didn't have much interest in the food distribution industry prior to the ride-along. She pursued the opportunity out of curiosity, but during the job shadow, what she saw and experienced intrigued her. As she told us later, it showed her what the actual job looked like, and she realized she would enjoy it. Now, having completed her internship with the company, she is working for them full time.

KEEP TRACK OF WHAT YOU LEARNED

This is where your job shadow pays off. As soon as the experience is over, take some time to think about everything you learned, then write it all down.

Break this information into a few categories, such as:

- The best advice I received
- What I would change or do differently at the company
- How to prepare for this career

Don't forget to do this step! It doesn't take long to forget what you heard, saw, and experienced. If you do a good job keeping track of the lessons you learned, you can combine notes from all of your job shadow experiences and use them to inform your launch criteria and career launch.

DELIVERABLES TO SELF

1. Develop a prospect list of five professionals that you might want to shadow. Anytime you meet someone in your chosen career field whom you think might be good to shadow, make note of their name and contact information. When you're ready to shadow someone, pull out the list and contact them.
2. Schedule your first job shadow. Don't keep putting it off. Follow the steps in this chapter, find a prospect, and make contact. Be respectful but bold. If you've begun developing a list of prospects, it will be much easier.
3. Develop a list of questions and topics you'd like to discuss during your job shadow. Keep this list in an easily accessible location, such as your laptop, so you can refine the questions over time.

13

PROFESSIONALISM

A Launcher got hired by a rather prestigious company, and as part of the training program, all new recruits were invited to a happy hour cocktail party. This gave recruits the opportunity to mix and mingle with company leaders, including the entire C-suite of executives.

During the event, the adult beverages flowed freely, and the Launcher proceeded to get absolutely hammered. This culminated in her running across the room and jumping on top of one of her friends, tackling her to the ground in front of the CEO, the CFO, and the COO. She made a big crash and a big scene, and it got her fired for unprofessional behavior.

In a single moment, with a single outburst of embarrassing behavior, a great career opportunity was lost. Many states are right-to-work states, so a company can let you go for any reason. If you do something stupid, embarrassing, or unprofessional, they will gladly give you the opportunity to go work for someone else.

WHAT IS PROFESSIONALISM?

Professionalism is a requirement for any Launcher, and it doesn't usually get taught in college. Not knowing how to behave professionally has been the downfall of many well-meaning young recruits, and it can be a major hindrance in successfully launching your career. There's usually an assumption that Launchers know what it means to behave professionally, but we want you to hold yourself to a higher standard.

If you've already been in the workforce and you're looking to start over, you probably already know what professionalism looks like. Then again, it may be the reason you're relaunching your career, in which case, this is your opportunity to get it right.

Professionalism is defined as the behavior that is expected of you as an employee—both in the workplace and outside of it. Many Launchers have been shocked to learn that doing something irresponsible outside of work can still get you fired.

While there's no comprehensive list of dos and don'ts, there are some key principles that can help you get it right. As in so many parts of your career launch, emotional intelligence plays a vital role in making sound judgments.

YOUR WORKDAY RESPONSIBILITIES

You may already have an idea about what your workday is going to look like. You probably envision a nine-to-five experience in an office setting. However, with the rise of collaborative internet platforms, many people are now working full time from home. If you're launching into a sales position, you might spend a lot of time alone on the road as you travel to meet with customers.

We find that many Launchers are shocked to discover that their work week isn't like a traditional nine-to-five office experience at all. They find themselves typing away late into the night, preparing proposals for clients and thinking, "I didn't know the days could be so long."

The line between being on the clock and off the clock has blurred, thanks to the accessibility provided by the internet and smartphones. It is now more likely for work life to cross into your non-work life. That's just the reality of being a professional today. It would be nice to think that as soon as you leave work for home, you're on your own time, but this may not be the case, depending on your industry and chosen field.

It is easy for employers to think your own time is no longer your own time, so how you behave, what you post, how you treat people, and what you say matters all the time. Just because you're not on the clock doesn't mean your bad behavior won't affect your job. In fact, there have been numerous stories in the media in the last few years of people losing their jobs due to inappropriate behavior being caught on camera. Company leaders didn't say, "They were on their own time, so we can't fire them." On the contrary, their behavior was viewed as a reflection of the company, even though they weren't representing the company at the time.

We like to tell Launchers, "Don't do anything you wouldn't want your grandmother to read about on the front page of your hometown newspaper."

RESPECT YOUR BOSS

You will be expected to show proper respect to your boss and the authority they wield over you. This seems to be a struggle for many young people. We heard a story about a manager who approached a young analyst and gave him his deliverables for thirty, sixty, and ninety-day deadlines.

There was one particular assignment—a financial analysis—that was particularly important for upper-level management to review at the end of the quarter, and the boss wanted it by the first deadline. After thirty days, however, the financial analysis wasn't done. When sixty days passed, the employee still hadn't completed it. Finally, the ninety-day deadline arrived, and the manager confronted him.

"Why didn't you get the financial analysis done?" he asked. "You completed all of the other work I assigned you. What happened?"

The young analyst turned to him, shrugged, and said, "I just didn't think it was that important."

Let us be blunt. In term of prioritization, it doesn't matter what you think. If your boss assigns you a task, project, or position, you don't get to assign your own level of importance to it. You are expected to get it done within the time frame they give you.

EATING, DRINKING, AND SOCIAL CONVERSATION

If you had helicopter parents, then their lives revolved around you, and they scheduled, managed, and guided almost every aspect of your life. Once you enter the workforce, you're going to learn the hard way that the world no longer revolves around you.

You're not in Kansas anymore, Toto. You are entering an established workplace culture, one you have identified you would enjoy, and it's up to you to fit into that culture because it's not going to conform itself to you. As a major part of that adjustment, you have to learn to adjust your social behavior to the expectations of those around you. We strongly encourage you to learn how to fit in as soon as possible.

Of course, you don't have to sell your soul by adopting unethical behavior, but try to fully embrace the company culture. Remember, they were getting along just fine before you got there, and they will continue to get along fine if you don't make it.

HOW TO BEHAVE AT MEALS

Learning how to behave at your company includes a lot of the social behaviors you might not think about. If a client, supervisor, or some other professional invites you to lunch or dinner, be mindful of the price point on the menu. If they are hosting the meal, they will probably order first, so pay attention to what they order. This will give you some clue about the implied budget. If they order a salad, you probably shouldn't order a filet mignon with a side of lobster bisque and cheesecake for dessert.

Picking up on subtle social cues will save you from a lot

of potential embarrassment in the workplace. Also, make sure you have a basic understanding of etiquette. If you are invited to a nice restaurant, do you know which silverware to use for each dish? Did you dress appropriately? Do you remember not to put your elbows on the table? You might think none of this should matter, but it makes an impact. If you're not sure how to act at a fancy dinner, take an etiquette class. Having nice manners can serve you well in a professional environment.

DRINKING ON THE JOB

There are going to be professional situations where alcohol is available. If the event is being hosted by someone else, follow their example. If they don't order a drink, don't order a drink. If they do, feel free to order something, but you don't have to. It might be a good idea to avoid drinking alcohol during a professional meeting altogether. At the very least, limit your intake. Even if there's an open bar and it seems like a casual, "fun" event, we recommend a hard limit of two drinks. Remember, you're not there to party. You're there to make a good impression—always.

DEALING WITH ETHICAL DILEMMAS

There may be times when your company asks you to do things you don't feel comfortable doing. Maybe they ask you to lie to a client, to fudge statistics, to play "fast and loose" with the truth, or to look the other way about some questionable activity. Or they may simply ask you to participate in something that is against your beliefs. It can be tricky to know how to deal with these kinds of situations.

If you work for a company and your personal ethics don't line up with the company's ethics, you're going to find yourself in uncomfortable situations. To avoid this, it is best to learn as much as you can about the company culture before you accept a position with them. Make sure it lines up with your personal values.

For example, we have some students whose strong Christian faith means they don't want to work on church holidays. It bothers their conscience to work on Sundays or Christmas or Good Friday. If that's important to them, they need to be sure they aren't taking a position at a company that's going to require them to work against their personal morality. It's not the company's responsibility to accommodate their personal conscience.

On the other hand, if a company is asking you to do things that are clearly illegal, then you have a hard choice to make. Should you continue to work there? At some point, you might have to walk away, as hard as that is. Ideally, you figure this out before you accept the job offer, but it doesn't always work out that way. We know that hindsight is twenty-twenty. A corrupt company will show its true colors in time. When that happens, it may be best to make a graceful exit. Nobody looks good in an orange jumpsuit.

There are going to be times when you're tempted to do unethical things to gain an advantage on the job. Resist the urge. One of our Launchers works for a chemical company. In the past, the company used to give chemical samples to potential customers as a way of trying to win them over. It was an effective sales tactic, but the cost added up.

Eventually, like most companies in the industry, the company stopped providing free samples. However, a few salespeople continued giving them. Essentially, they were stealing chemicals from the company to give to customers as "free" samples. Our former student gave away hundreds of gallons before he got caught. When leaders threatened to fire him, he said, "I'm just doing what the company has always done."

"We stopped giving away free samples eight years ago," they replied, "and we were very clear about it. You chose to ignore our explicit instructions to give yourself a sales advantage, and you've cost the company a lot of money in the process."

Needless to say, his time at the company came to an end that day.

Another former student found himself caught in an unethical situation when the executives at his company decided to move forward on a deal after receiving inside information. Though this was potentially illegal, the CEO didn't think they would get caught.

The former student ultimately decided to walk away. "I'm not going to risk going to jail, not even for a nice amount of money," he said. In fact, he left millions on the table, but he also avoided putting himself at risk of losing everything.

No matter the industry, you are going to find yourself dealing with ethical dilemmas from time to time, whether from temptations, shady business practices, personal moral failings, or the questionable behavior of company leaders. We strongly urge you to act aboveboard at all times in all situations. It's just not worth it to cross the line.

BEHAVIOR AT COMPANY MEETINGS

As soon as you accept a job offer, your company is going to begin inviting you to company meetings of various kinds. Even if some of these meetings are boring as heck, you need to maintain a level of professionalism that sets you apart. If the company hires a keynote speaker, pay attention. Resist the all-too-common urge to check your phone. In fact, we've found that having your phone on your desk will make you at least fifteen percent less productive. Keep it in your pocket on silent.

Let's be brutally honest. Some keynote speakers are more boring than watching paint dry. It doesn't matter. Pay attention and try to glean something from what they say. Otherwise, you are, in a sense, wasting company money. It's your job to listen.

We often have CEOs and company leaders speak to our sales class, and even with an excellent speaker, we are amazed at how many students will sit there preoccupied on their phone. Sometimes, the student will tell us afterward, "Well, the speaker wasn't from my industry, so I didn't think I needed to pay attention."

This is completely missing the point. It does not matter who it is. Every speaker has something meaningful or useful to offer you, even if their area of expertise isn't directly relevant. Secondly, and more importantly, learning to pay attention and stay engaged is both professional and ethical. It's a skill you're going to need if you want to succeed, so you might as well practice it.

Your goal is to reflect well on your company and on yourself. Some behaviors that might be okay in a casual relationship don't belong in the professional world. We know of a Launcher who had a running joke with his supervisor. They tended to use the restroom at the same time every day at work, so they often joked about it.

One day, they were both in a meeting with the supervisor's boss, and the Launcher excused himself to use the bathroom. As he was walking to the door, he turned to his supervisor and said, "Hey, man, I'm going to the bathroom. Aren't you coming with me?"

This was simply part of the running joke, but in that particular situation, it completely embarrassed the supervisor in front of his boss. It made him look foolish, and it was just awkward.

OWN YOUR OUTCOMES

There's a great book called *Extreme Ownership* by Jocko Willink and Leif Babin. Although the book is about the Navy SEALs, some of the principles they offer are broadly applicable to all people. One of the things they say is, "You're not a victim of circumstance." In other words, you are in a situation because you put yourself there. If you're late for work, accept that it's because you didn't get up early enough. If you missed a deadline, accept that it's because you procrastinated.

The idea is to take ownership of your outcomes. Even if outside circumstances influence the end result, you ultimately bear responsibility for your own actions. Own your mistakes and take responsibility for correcting them. Don't make excuses or blame others. You're not the victim.

As you approach your career launch, just remember that *everything you do* in the presence of company representatives, no matter the venue or occasion, will become part of the information they use to evaluate you. This continues to be the case after your career launch.

Your reputation follows you. It doesn't matter if you move industries. Word gets around, so always behave responsibly, respectably, and ethically.

RECOMMENDED READING

Extreme Ownership: How US Navy SEALs Lead and Win by Jocko Willink and Leif Babin

Grit: The Power of Passion and Perseverance by Angela Duckworth

TRAVEL

Travel is fatal to prejudice, bigotry, and narrow-mindedness, and many of our people need it sorely on these accounts. Broad, wholesome, charitable views of men and things cannot be acquired by vegetating in one little corner of the earth all one's lifetime.

—MARK TWAIN, *THE INNOCENTS ABROAD*

Travel is an important part of almost any professional career, yet it has also been responsible for thousands of broken marriages. It's not easy being away from home, from a spouse or kids, and it can cause disappointment with your job and even your overall career.

We deal with this a lot in our program at Texas A&M because our focus is on sales. Some salespeople enjoy this aspect of the job. They love visiting other cities, meeting customers in their offices, learning about local cultures, and having their eyes opened to a wider variety of experiences. Others absolutely *hate* being away from home. For them, it might be the worst aspect of their career. However, even if you're not interested in sales, there's a good chance you will end up doing a bit of traveling for your professional career.

YOUR EXPERIENCE WILL VARY

Your experience with on-the-job travel will vary considerably depending on your industry, company, and specific position. If you're doing outside sales in the lumber industry, you might regularly travel around a one-hundred-and-fifty-mile territory in order to call on customers, but you will be back home every night. You will probably have a company car, which you can also use for personal travel, saving you as much as a thousand dollars a month on expenses (gas, insurance, upkeep, repairs). Instead of a company car, you might receive a travel allowance.

If you're a consultant or financial analyst working for a large, international corporation, you might have to travel out of town for several days at a time. For a single Launcher with no constraints, this kind of travel might be appealing. For others, it can spell disaster for their personal lives. Your significant other might not appreciate you being gone constantly.

Travel paid for by the company is an excellent way to see the world if you enjoy the lifestyle. Some companies create strict agendas for employees when they travel, but others are quite generous. A company might give you an afternoon or even a couple of extra days to play golf, go fishing, or see the sights.

Just be sure to clarify a company's travel policy before deciding to work for them. Make sure it will be compatible with your life and personality. While technology has made travel less burdensome for families, providing more ways than ever to keep in touch, it might still be hard on loved ones.

HOW COMMON IS PROFESSIONAL TRAVEL?

You might love the idea of traveling. You might even have a wanderlust mentality. On the other hand, you might be more of a homebody. Maybe you haven't done much travel, and you're not sure how you feel about it.

We find that many people in their twenties love seeing the world. They would rather invest money in experiences than material possessions. However, there are those who are perfectly happy living their whole lives in West, Texas, or some other tiny town. Whatever your preferences, we recommend at least being *open* to the idea of working in a career that requires some travel.

While it's fine to live in a small town your whole life, in many industries you will limit your upward mobility if you're unwilling to go anywhere. Your current position might not require you to leave town, but higher-level positions in a major company will almost always have some kind of regular travel, whether to attend conferences, visit company headquarters, or meet with clients around the world. If you aspire to become a VP, CEO, CFO or some other high-level executive, occasional travel will become absolutely imperative.

Sam Walton was an Arkansas country boy, born and raised, but he spent a lot of his time flying across the country in his single-engine plane, scouting locations for Walmart stores. Much to the chagrin of the FAA, he didn't always get clearance before buzzing local airports with his private plane and landing in the countryside where he thought a Walmart distribution center might be located.

Even if you're satisfied staying in a low-level position, you might be required to travel. For example, we have a student working as a vehicle salesman at an auto dealer in San Antonio, and his employer told the sales team, "I want you to visit dealerships around the country so you can pick up some ideas about how we should deal with customers."

MAKE IT WORK FOR YOU

Penny and Terrell are two students who graduated almost fifteen years ago. They planned to get married soon after graduation, and their intention was to spend every single day (and night) together for the rest of their lives. To achieve this personal goal, they decided to launch a software company right here in College Station, designing and selling software for cattle farmers around the world.

The only days they spend away from home are when they go to trade shows, but they are *never* apart. They have made millions of dollars selling software to customers in forty countries, and they've kept their word to each other.

They knew what their needs and goals were in regard to travel (or, specifically, the lack of travel), and they chose a career path that aligned with their desires. They didn't just stumble into a career and struggle with professional travel requirements they hadn't anticipated.

Dr. Litzenberg has twin daughters, both of whom are highly successful in their careers. One daughter is the principal of a local school, has an eleven-year-old child, and almost never travels, except for occasional workshops. The other daughter lives in a suburb of Houston near the airport and travels constantly. She's the vice president of people for a private equity firm that owns numerous restaurant franchises, and she visits franchises across the country regularly. She has a husband and two daughters, but they make it work for their family.

When she has time off, she uses her frequent flyer miles to take her family on fun vacations, and her husband is supportive of her career. He works with her to keep the house running smoothly, and they have a strong relationship. It might not work for other families, but it works for them. That's the key.

We had a student in our program last year who expressed reservations about becoming a professional salesperson. When we talked to her about it, she explained that she was worried about the travel. Her chosen industry was medical device sales, but she couldn't imagine driving all over Texas in her car to meet with hospital clinic managers. It didn't appeal to her at all, and that's fine. She was smart enough to avoid a career that would have made her miserable.

YOU MIGHT LOVE IT

On the other hand, some Launchers who are initially hesitant to embrace a career that will take them far from home later learn they love it. Trey graduated twenty years ago and went to work for a multinational chemical company. At the time, Trey and his wife told Dr. Litzenberg they weren't into traveling and intended to live in Fredericksburg, a small town in central Texas, for the rest of their lives.

Dr. Litzenberg lost track of Trey for a number of years until a surprise encounter at an industry conference in Parma, Italy. He was surprised to see Trey at an international meeting and asked him where lived.

"My wife and I live in Switzerland now," Trey said. "We've traveled all over Europe on business, and Switzerland was our favorite place."

Dr. Litzenberg couldn't believe it. "The last time we talked, you both intended to stay in Fredericksburg forever."

"That was before I knew how wonderful it was to live in Switzerland," Trey said. "We have a multistory chateau on a lake. We didn't know where we really belonged because we hadn't experienced the world yet."

PRINCIPLES OF PROFESSIONAL TRAVEL

Maybe you've done a bit of traveling already, or maybe it's all new to you. If you're a Relauncher, you probably have some experience under your belt. However, we have many students who have never been more than a few miles away from home. They have no idea what long-distance travel is like, much less the professional travel experiences of an ambitious careerist.

Whatever your situation, there are some key principles to keep in mind as you prepare for your career launch.

LEARN THE TRAVEL REQUIREMENTS OF YOUR CAREER

Most careers, and most jobs, have some expectation that you will travel occasionally on work-related business. You may not experience this during the first few months on the job. In fact, the first few months are rarely a good indicator of what your normal, ongoing experience at a company is going to be like. At other companies, travel begins almost immediately, as Launchers are sent for training at far-flung locations.

Some large corporations have intensive training programs that occur in special facilities. They spare no expense, bringing in industry experts to teach you the science and specifics of each product or service. If that's the case, you could be traveling hundreds of miles to the training facility.

Whatever the case, make sure you know exactly what you're getting into. Address the travel requirements of a job offer in the early stages of the interview process.

If it's not mentioned in the job description, you will have to ask directly, "How much travel is expected with this position?"

You might also ask how much travel will be required to become upwardly mobile in the company. An entry-level position might not require you to go anywhere, but that might not be the case once you've climbed a few rungs on the ladder. You need to know so you can make an informed decision about the opportunity.

If you don't want to travel, don't accept an offer that will require it. If travel is mentioned in the job description, don't even ask for an interview. If you're fine with some travel, make sure you know exactly what to expect. Match your travel expectation to your launch criteria.

ASK SPECIFICALLY ABOUT OVERNIGHT TRAVEL

In particular, you need to know how often you're going to be away from home at night because this is the aspect of travel that makes the biggest impact on your personal life. The job description might mention travel but neglect to mention how much of it will require being away from home overnight. Make sure it won't damage the relationships that matter most to you. Frequent on-the-job travel can wreck a marriage if your spouse isn't fine with it.

MATCH TRAVEL EXPECTATIONS WITH YOUR PREFERRED LIFESTYLE

You've no doubt heard or read discussions about the importance of work-life balance, but have you considered what this looks like for you? Some people thrive in a job where they work sixty hours a week. It feels balanced to them. Some have no problem balancing frequent work travel with a healthy personal life. What does work-life balance mean for you?

Technology has made the separation of frequent travel a little less traumatic than it used to be. We have a friend in the National Guard who did an eighteen-month tour of duty in Iraq. Being away from her two small children was difficult, but the military provided a satellite link that allowed her to chat with them every night. In the middle of a war zone, sitting in a tent, she would read a book to them every night.

It wasn't as good as being with them in person, but it helped make the time away bearable. You have access to social media, video chat, and other means of communication that might make traveling away from family more acceptable. Unlike past decades, you don't have to worry about the long-distance fee when you phone home. You've got FaceTime, Skype, and so many other options. Is it enough for you? Only you can decide.

MAKE SURE YOUR LOVED ONES UNDERSTAND YOUR TRAVEL REQUIREMENTS

Your significant other and any immediate family members deserve to know how much you're going to be traveling. They might not ask, so you will have to bring it up. If it's a deal-breaker for the relationship, then you might want to think long and hard about accepting the position.

A friend of ours spent fifteen years on the road selling supplies to veterinarians. His wife was a stay-at-home mom, but she often felt like she was a single mom because he was gone so often.

Finally, she confronted him. "This isn't working," she said. "Either you divorce your company, or you divorce me."

"I'll figure out a way to be at home more often," he replied.

The next day, he quit and found another job that required very little travel. Now, he's home all the time, and his marriage is much stronger for it.

When it comes to work travel, the priorities of your spouse or partner matter. Communicate your expected travel requirements with them *before* you accept a job offer. Make sure they are okay with it.

We know of one woman who takes her kids and their

nanny with her when she travels for work. The nanny watches the kids during the day, and the woman spends quality time with them in the evening. You don't have to be home every night to be a great spouse, partner, mom, or dad, but you don't want to miss out on life's most important moments. If it matters to you, you can make it work.

INCLUDE TRAVEL IN YOUR LAUNCH CRITERIA

When you first created your launch criteria list back in Chapter Six, you might not have included your travel preferences. Hopefully, you've now begun to think about it. Add it to the list and weight it accordingly.

What aspects of travel matter most do you? Is it important to be home every night? Do you want to be able to unplug completely when you're with your family? Whatever your criteria regarding travel, add them to your list now.

DELIVERABLES TO SELF

It's possible that you've never thought about travel as part of your career. If so, it's time to start. Spend some quiet time pondering your own feelings about traveling professionally. How do you feel about a job that requires you to travel around your local area every day but allows you to be home at night? How do you feel about a job that occasionally sends you to other cities, even other countries? How do you feel about a job that sends you around the world regularly?

Spend some time *this week* talking to your spouse, partner, and family about on-the-job travel. How would travel affect your relationships with them?

In the end, attempt to arrive at a specific *percentage* that you're comfortable with. For example, you might decide, "I would be okay if travel was thirty percent of my job." If you're not sure, then we recommend finding a job shadow opportunity that includes some travel. See for yourself what it's like and learn from someone who is already dealing with it.

As you implement these deliverables to self and figure out exactly where you stand on career travel, check off the following steps (but only if they're true). If you're not there yet, leave them blank and return to them later.

____ I have a clear idea of how much I would like to travel in my career.

____ I have settled on a percentage of the time that I'm comfortable traveling in my career.

____ I have spoken to my significant other and learned how they feel about my career travel requirements.

START READING *TODAY*

I read and think, so I do more reading and thinking, and make fewer impulse decisions than most people in business. I do it because I like this kind of life.

—WARREN BUFFETT

We have between twenty and twenty-five industry representatives working with our students every semester. In twenty years of running this program at Texas A&M, that means we've had *hundreds* of professionals speak to our students and share their advice for career success, and one quality that every single one of them has shared is a *penchant for reading.*

In our experience, most successful professionals read, and they read a lot. This is no coincidence. There's no other way to keep up professionally. In his ever-popular book *The 7 Habits of Highly Effective People*, Stephen Covey calls it "sharpening the saw." Reading keeps you motivated during the ho-hum work week. It keeps you abreast of the latest cutting-edge thinking from thought leaders in your industry. It helps you solve problems or look at things in a new way.

Over the years, Bill Gates has recommended a total of 186 books on his personal blog *Gates Notes*.[3] Despite being one of the most successful people in the world, he clearly still believes he has much to learn from others. More than that, he knows one of the best ways he can help others is to recommend great books.

In past decades, wealthy moguls like Howard Hughes or William Randolph Hurst were known for withdrawing into a cocoon of privilege and eccentricity. Some became philanthropists, but they tended to support things like art museums and their alma maters, things that benefited their own circle of privilege. Bill Gates, on the other hand, has devoted millions to helping the poorest of the poor. He's trying hard to make the world a better place, and his book recommendations are part of that effort.

Warren Buffett credits many of his best money decisions

3   Marcel Schwantes, "Bill Gates Reads 50 Books Per Year. But Only These 6 Leadership Books Made His List of Recommendations," *Inc.*, June 8, 2018, https://www.inc.com/marcel-schwantes/bill-gates-reads-50-books-per-year-but-only-these-6-leadership-books-made-his-list-of-recommendations.html.

to his voracious reading habit. He estimates that he spends as much as eighty percent of his day reading. He starts every morning by poring over several newspapers. In an article in the *Motley Fool*, Matthew Frankel writes, "When asked about his secrets to success, Buffett once pointed at a stack of books and said: 'Read five hundred pages like this every day. That's how knowledge works. It builds up, like compound interest.'"[4]

Self-made millionaire Steve Siebold, author of *How Rich People Think*, has interviewed more than twelve hundred of the world's wealthiest people in the last thirty years to discover what traits they have in common. One of those traits? They read everything from self-improvement books to autobiographies.

Author Thomas Corley spent five years studying the daily activities of 233 rich people and 128 poor people, which he wrote about in *Rich Habits: The Daily Success Habits of Wealthy Individuals*. He found that sixty-seven percent of rich people limited TV time to one hour or less per day, compared to only twenty-three percent of poor people.

The next time you reach for the TV remote, you might want to reconsider. Crack open a book instead.

---

4   Matthew Frankel, "Your 2018 Warren Buffett Book List," *The Motley Fool*, May 15, 2018, https://www.fool.com/investing/2018/05/15/your-2018-warren-buffett-book-list.aspx.

EXPAND YOUR HORIZONS

Once you realize the fantastic *resource* that books provide for your career, it changes your perspective. No longer are books merely assignments given by teachers. No longer are they drudgery. The lightbulb turns on, and you realize they are contributing to your success.

Reading increases your emotional intelligence. It increases your knowledge. It broadens your perspective, expands your horizons, and hastens your personal and professional development. You become a lifelong learner. Leaders are readers.

Read often. Read well.

To become a regular reader and lifelong learner, there are some principles you must embrace.

COMMIT YOURSELF TO PROFESSIONAL DEVELOPMENT BY READING

We believe reading is absolutely essential for professional development, so when choosing something to read, pick things that will keep you "in the know." We've recommended some excellent reading throughout this book, so do yourself a favor and take advantage of what they have to offer. You will be richly rewarded. You can also ask your mentors for book recommendations. Chances are they'll have a few that have meant a lot to them.

No matter where you are in your career launch journey, start your professional reading today. It's what practically *all* successful professionals do. You might feel like you're too busy to read. That's understandable, but it's not entirely true. Break down the actual hours of your week, and you'll find plenty of available hours. There are 168 hours in a week. How many of those do you spend sleeping? How many do you spend in class? How many do you spend doing necessary work—homework, a part-time job, and other responsibilities?

Subtract all of your busy hours from the weekly total and see if you can come up with even just one uncommitted hour that you could spend reading. When we have students do this exercise, many of them wind up with twenty or thirty hours of free time a week. All we're saying is grab a book during one of those available hours. No matter your age, your career stage, or your knowledge base, you have much to learn from others.

EXPLORE ALTERNATE WAYS OF GETTING INFORMATION

If you don't enjoy reading books, there are alternate ways

to get the same information. We recommend either listening to audiobooks or using a summary service.

Summary services glean the key insights from popular books and distill them down into a more digestible format. A book that might take hours to read can be summarized into a twenty-minute text or audio format. Instaread.com and Summary.com are two of the more popular services, and most of the best-selling business book titles are available on either website. With these services, you can quickly devour the meatiest information from a business book during your commute or on your lunch break.

Personally, we're fond of audiobooks. You can listen to them on a long commute, during a drive home, or during a road trip. Audible is the most popular audiobook service, and you get two free books just for signing up.

You can also read shorter content, such as articles. There are many great industry-related websites releasing a steady stream of content from successful men and woman in the form of short articles and opinion pieces.

READ FOR FUN

Reading isn't merely a burden you must take on in order to learn new things. It's also a great way to have fun, unwind, and destress from a busy day. You might be a very slow reader. That's fine. In fact, we find it helpful to read one chapter, then pause and think about it for a while. You don't have to rush through or devour hundreds of pages in one sitting. Take it at a pace that allows you to actually enjoy the experience.

DELIVERABLES TO SELF

1. The next time you pass by a bookstore, take a moment, head inside, and pick up a book. Even if you prefer ebooks or audiobooks, there's something magical about holding that printed paper copy in your hands. Read the back cover copy and see if anything jumps out at you or makes you think, "This sounds like some information that I could benefit from." We've found that this simple exercise can provide a little boost of motivation to get people reading.

2. Take a couple of minutes each week to jot down some ideas or insights you gleaned from authors you've read recently. Too often, people will finish a book, say, "That was pretty good," then set it aside and never think about it again. When you do that, you run the risk of losing valuable information you picked up. This week, begin the habit of thinking through what you've read, taking note of the insights you found most helpful or interesting, and writing them down.

3. Combine those key insights into a working document

of the books you've read. This will help you remember where you got certain ideas in case you need to return to them. It will also make it easier to recommend specific books to others.

4. In that working document, include a list of books you *want* to read. When you get a recommendation, add the title and author to the list so you don't forget it. Even if the list gets incredibly long, it will ensure that you're never in a situation where you say, "I should read something, but I don't know what."

THE BEST-LAID PLANS OF MICE AND MEN

In the previous fifteen chapters, we've covered all the major steps to preparing for your career launch. At this point, you know what you need to do over the next few months to get ready. Keep working through the exercises we've offered. Refer back to the chapters as you develop and implement your plan.

In the coming chapters, we're going to discuss some essential principles for successfully navigating your career. From overcoming negative self-talk to quitting a job to dealing with intergenerational conflicts, these principles will continue to be important throughout your career. However, you don't have to wait until you launch your career to read these chapters. The concepts we discuss will already begin making a difference during your launch preparations.

> **RECOMMENDED READING**
>
> The 7 Habits of Highly Effective People by Stephen Covey
>
> How Rich People Think by Steve Siebold
>
> Rich Habits: The Daily Success Habits of Wealthy Individuals by Thomas Corley

PART FOUR

SUCCESS IN THE WORKPLACE

MOVING FROM NEGATIVE SELF-TALK AND DOUBT TO CONFIDENCE

It has been said that we think about sixty thousand thoughts a day. Whether or not that number is accurate, research has found that we tend to think the *same* thoughts over and over again.[5] These thought patterns cause us to develop specific, personal assumptions that influence how we feel physically, mentally, and emotionally.

What impact is your constant mental chatter having on your well-being? Is negative self-talk keeping you from

---

[5] Robert Leahy, "Is Dwelling on the Negative Hurting You? The Cognitive Costs of Rumination," *Life: The Blog*, December 30, 2010, https://www.huffpost.com/entry/dwelling-on-the-negative_b_799103.

being productive? Is that little voice inside your head limiting your career, relationships, and self-confidence? Left unchecked, your inner critic can be the most destructive force in your life.

In this chapter, we want to help you recognize the negative self-talk that might be hindering your career or career launch so you can bolster your self-confidence. It's time to break the hold of that inner critic and become your best self. To do that, we recommend a few specific activities and healthy habits.

TALKING YOURSELF INTO A WORST-CASE SCENARIO

A career launch often brings with it a lot of doubt and fear because you are moving into a new arena where you have less confidence in your abilities. At this point, you should have mentors who are helping you to learn and grow, but you have to take this external help and begin to internalize it.

Dr. Litzenberg took one of his favorite Launchers—his daughter—to a car dealership so she could buy a new vehicle. She had recently gone through a divorce, and she was trying to relaunch her life. However, as they walked across the parking lot, she kept up a steady stream of negative self-talk. "We probably won't find a car. I probably won't have good enough credit. The divorce probably ruined my credit. The dealer will probably try to rip me off. I'll probably wind up with a clunker."

Finally, he stopped and turned to her. "That's it," he said. "This negative talk has to stop. You have to approach this with a little confidence. You have money, so you have the power here. They want to make a sale, so they aren't going to turn you away. You're trying to talk yourself into a worst-case scenario. Stop that."

We see this with Launchers all too often. A student will tell us on a Friday afternoon, "I have a job interview on Monday, but I have to go home this weekend. I won't have time to prepare, so the interview will probably be a disaster. Plus, my best suit hasn't come back from the cleaners. Maybe I don't even want this job anyway."

You might not even be aware of the steady stream of self-defeating talk because it has become second nature to you. However, it has a direct, negative impact on how you act, react, and interact with people and situations. Nothing is more catastrophic in a person's life than the steady drumbeat of negative self-talk. Nothing.

We had a student with the interesting name of Mary Margaret Miller in our customer relationship management class. Much of the curriculum focuses on emotional intelligence and understanding your own emotional triggers. One day, Mary mentioned that she'd scheduled an interview with the agricultural services company Cargill, but when she told us about it, she said, "I have this interview with Cargill, but I'm probably not going to get it. There's no way I'll be good enough. I should probably just move back to my hometown and get a sales job."

We had to counter this inner critic by reminding her that she's smart, talented, and has real potential to impress the interviewer. However, it took several weeks of working with her before we could root out the negative self-talk completely. There was a constant inner dialogue telling her to give up and move back home. She was from a small town that's about twenty miles from campus physically, but about ten thousand miles socially, and she was convinced she would wind up there again.

She finally broke free of the doubt, and when her interview with Cargill happened, she nailed it. In fact, she did so well that she became the number one interviewee in the nation for that internship. Cargill is one of the largest companies in the world, so that's quite an accomplishment. She had the potential all along, but she had to see it in herself before she could approach the interview with the necessary amount of confidence to be her best self.

Confidence was vital to her success because Cargill's

interview process is fairly intense. Recruits complete six different interviews in front of multiple recruiters who barrage them with questions and then grade their performance and responses. In the end, Mary scored the highest in the nation.

As the old saying goes, "If you always do what you've always done, you always get what you've always gotten." Can you imagine how much worse she would have done if her inner critic had been constantly dragging her down during the interview process? She's now doing an internship with Cargill and having a great experience, and confidence made it possible.

WHAT YOU SAY TO YOURSELF MATTERS

You wouldn't be friends with someone who spoke to you the way you speak to yourself. Let that sink in. Would you want to spend time with a person who constantly told you that you're fat, stupid, and destined to fail? Would you enjoy the company of someone who told you that you look ugly every time you put on a dress or suit?

Of course not, so why in the world do you do it to yourself? Studies have shown that negative self-talk creates high levels of anxiety, stress, and depression, so there's a real danger that it can become a self-fulfilling prophecy.[6]

---

6   Elizabeth Scott, "The Toxic Effects of Negative Self-Talk," *Very Well Mind*, December 10, 2018, https://www.verywellmind.com/negative-self-talk-and-how-it-affects-us-4161304.

What if, instead of constantly knocking yourself down, you were always building yourself up? We're not talking about being arrogant or cocky. We're talking about creating a constant stream of encouragement, hope, and positivity. What would that do for you? How would a massive boost in confidence impact your studies, your relationships, your work? This requires a huge shift in your mindset because your inner critic has the force of many years of habit, and we all know how hard it can be to break a bad habit. At first, you're going to have to counter the negativity with intentionality.

When your inner critic says, "You're not going to pass this test," you have to stop yourself and counter it, "I know I need to study, but I can do this." When you have a big project that is due soon, your inner critic might say, "You'll never get it done on time." You can counter it by saying, "I know I sometimes procrastinate, but I can get this done on time if I work hard."

When you're new on the job, that inner critic is going to be more active than ever. "You're no good at this job. You don't know what you're doing. Everyone else is better than you." Counter it by reminding yourself, "I'm new in this company, and it's going to take some time to get up to the same level as the people who've already been working here, but I know I have talents and skills I can use to get there. I have what I need to be successful."

If you tend to run late, instead of beating yourself up—"I'm always late for work. I never get anywhere on time. What's wrong with me?"—you can try some intentional encouragement, like, "I'm running late again today, but I'm going to work on this. I will leave the house a little earlier tomorrow."

GIVE YOURSELF ROOM TO FAIL

You're not going to be perfect at everything, so give yourself room (and permission) to fail. According to HGTV star Chip Gaines, "Fear dressed up as wisdom provides poor counsel."[7] Look at failure as an opportunity to learn and grow, to get out of your comfort zone and push yourself just a little harder.

Acknowledge it, stare it in the face, give your failure a great big hug and say, "Thanks for the opportunity to learn." Then walk away knowing that you've gained valuable experience. There's a lot of pressure on you to be the best—from yourself, from others—but you can't respond to failure, even a big failure, as the end of everything. Very few failures are truly catastrophic. In most instances, you can recover. If anything, a failure is just evidence that you're not stagnant, caught in the ordinary, or going through the motions.

---

7   Chip Gaines (@chipgaines), Twitter, October 17, 2017, https://twitter.com/chipgaines/status/920333188756660224.

Growing up in West Texas, Codie often heard the old saying, "If you fall off the horse, climb back on and try again." If you let the inner critic beat you up every time you fail, you suppress your own development, make yourself timid and afraid to try new things, and hinder your own creative expression. When you give yourself room to fail, you open the door to creativity, growth, and self-discovery.

TRIGGERING THE INNER CRITIC

Earlier, we mentioned the importance of recognizing your own emotional triggers. It's also important to recognize those things that trigger the negative self-talk within you. Typically, we struggle with negative self-talk when we step outside of our comfort zone. Does it happen when you're working out, while you're taking a test, when you're attempting to network with other industry people, or when you're giving a presentation at an important meeting? By identifying your triggers, you can more effectively counter the inner critic with positivity and diminish its terrible effect on you.

Maybe you have an emotional trigger related to money. You might have an emotional trigger related to an ex-spouse. When someone mentions the name of a former boyfriend, it might immediately put you in a bad frame of mind. Whatever the case, you need to recognize your own emotional triggers so you can counteract the negative talk that they induce. This self-awareness is a vital part of emotional intelligence, and it will serve you well throughout your career.

When are you the hardest on yourself? What is it about that situation that makes the inner critic start putting you down? How might you counter the negativity by turning it into encouragement? It will take time to end this bad habit, but thinking through these questions will help you get started. In time, with practice, the inner critic can be transformed into an inner champion who is always cheering you on and encouraging you to get up when you fall.

As soon as you start feeling angry, anxious, depressed, or upset, stop and reflect on your state of mind. Before the inner critic can make the situation worse, take a step back and analyze the situation from an outsider's perspective. Are things really as bad, as hopeless, and as out of control as they seem?

Some psychologists recommend giving your inner critic a name, ideally a silly one, so you can deal with it directly. "Uh oh, Timmy's telling me how stupid I am again." Don't be afraid to confront Timmy and argue with him.

Here are some questions you can use to challenge Timmy the next time the negative self-talk begins:

REALITY CHECK QUESTIONS

- Am I jumping to conclusions?
- Is there evidence that supports the negative viewpoint?

PERSPECTIVE QUESTIONS

- What good can I find in this situation?
- If someone else was in my position, what would I say to encourage them?
- Does this really matter in the grand scheme of things?

ALTERNATIVE EXPLANATIONS

- How else can I look at this situation?
- If I were in a good mood, how would I look at this situation?

GOAL-ORIENTED QUESTIONS

- Is this way of thinking helping me achieve my goals?
- What can I learn from this situation to be better equipped next time?

AVOID SPEAKING IN ABSOLUTES

How many times do you use statements like the following?

- I always (insert negative action).

- I never (insert positive action).

In other words, "I'm always late. I never make it to work on time. I'm always falling behind. I never get caught up. I always do a terrible job. I'll never get it right."

The words *always* and *never* are a type of *cognitive distortion* called "all-or-nothing thinking," which is one of many ways your brain lies to you. It takes a real situation and shifts it to the extreme so that a disappointment becomes a total failure.

Always and *never* are easy to use, easy to comprehend, but impossible to quantify. People sometimes use them in arguments. Suppose you forgot to text your significant other about an important event. They feel insulted, so they express their emotions by saying, "You *always* forget to text me!" Realistically, of course, you only *sometimes* forget to text. You might even *frequently* forget to text.

The next time you're tempted to use one of these words in reference to something you've done, pause and try to put the situation into a realistic perspective. You were late to work this morning, but are you *always* late? That's what your inner critic says, but actually count the number of times in the last month when you were late. Suddenly, "I'm always late" becomes "I was late four times in the last month." With a more realistic perspective on the problem, it becomes easier to find a reasonable solution. "I'll set my alarm a few minutes earlier. Some of the tasks I do in the morning I will do the evening before instead."

CONGRATULATE YOURSELF

You have little moments of excellence in your everyday life. Start recognizing those moments, embracing them, and *congratulating* yourself. Bask in your success and accomplishments, no matter how small.

It's not arrogant or conceited to congratulate yourself. On the contrary, it challenges you to be more positive so you can enjoy life a little more, and it inspires you to strive for more and greater success. Find opportunities to encourage yourself every day, even if the task you complete isn't exciting. It might feel awkward at first, especially if you're used to being negative towards yourself, but push through the awkwardness.

Eventually, congratulating yourself will become a habit, and you will begin to notice an overall improvement in your self-esteem. You completed a two-mile run this morning? Give yourself a pat on the back. You got your to-do list done? Give yourself an "attaboy" or "attagirl." You got a B on the test instead of a C? Tell yourself, "Good job. We'll do *even better* next time."

Self-care is so important, but many Launchers under-value it. People will spend sixty dollars or more on a massage to work out their tension, but taking time to speak positively to yourself costs nothing and has just as big of an impact. Taking care of your mind and emotions is *at least* as important as taking care of your body, and once you develop a habit of positive self-talk, you will start to feel more confident.

CONFIDENCE, NOT ARROGANCE

Confidence is defined as "belief in one's self and one's ability to succeed."[8] It is often confused with self-esteem, which has more to do with loving and appreciating your-self. You need a healthy amount of both.

If you're able to get up in front of a crowd and give a speech, commanding the room, you have a lot of confidence. If you feel proud of yourself after giving your speech, that shows self-esteem.

You don't want to have so much of either that you overes-timate your abilities or fail at a task you underestimated. You're not going to be perfect at everything. Telling yourself, "I am going to the Olympics next year and get a perfect score on the balance beam," is probably not

8   "Confidence," *Psychology Today*, accessed January 14, 2019, https://www.psychologytoday. com/us/basics/confidence.

realistic or helpful. If you're overconfident, it's easy to overpromise and fail to complete tasks because you've taken on too much.

Still, we find a *lack* of confidence is the bigger and more common problem. We meet Launchers all the time who avoid taking risks that could lead to major success in school, at work, or in relationships because they're just not confident enough.

Finding a healthy balance will help you deal with pressure, make the most of every opportunity, gain credibility, make a great first impression, and overcome challenges. The biggest way to boost confidence is to put a stop to negative self-talk and begin encouraging yourself.

VISUALIZE YOURSELF SUCCEEDING

If you mentally walk through the steps to successfully complete a task, you will be more prepared when you face the situation. For example, if you have a job interview coming up, it can be helpful to work through the conversation in your head a few times in advance.

Olympic swimmer Michael Phelps used to *mentally rehearse* for two hours a day, recalling every detail of cutting through the water, turning on the wall, and speeding toward the finish line. According to his coach,

Bob Bowman, this regular visualization contributed to Phelps's success by preparing him for the decisions he would have to make once he was in the pool. He continues to use this practice in other areas of his life.[9]

We work with a woman who was at one time on the Olympic shooting team. She has told us that when she was training for the Olympics, she had three part-time coaches who worked with her. One focused on her shooting technique, another focused on her physical fitness, and a third focused on her mental sharpness. As it turns out, Olympic shooting is largely a mind game. You have to visualize the target and block everything else out, imagine your shot hitting the target, and keep your nerves steady.

She also gave herself frequent pep talks. Her mental coach also stayed with her throughout the day so he could keep her mind sharp and on task. She would be sitting at breakfast, in the middle of eating pancakes, and suddenly he would bark instructions at her.

"Visualize the target," he might say, even though she had a forkful of food halfway to her mouth. "Describe to me what you need to do to hit it."

9   Carmine Gallo, "3 Daily Habits of Peak Performers, According to Michael Phelps' Coach," *Forbes*, May 24, 2016, https://www.forbes.com/sites/carminegallo/2016/05/24/3-daily-habits-of-peak-performers-according-to-michael-phelps-coach.

WEAR CLOTHES THAT MAKE YOU FEEL PUT TOGETHER

This section might resonate more with the women reading this book, but studies have shown that it applies to everyone. Wearing clothes that make you feel better about yourself boosts your confidence. Codie used to dress up for tests because the extra confidence improved her performance, but the same technique works in job interviews, presentations, and networking events.

People perceive you differently when you are dressed well, but we also feel better about ourselves. Think about how you feel in a job interview when you're disheveled and wearing wrinkled clothes compared to how you feel when you're wearing a nice suit that you know makes you look good. When you're confident about your appearance, it influences your performance.

DON'T COMPARE YOURSELF TO OTHERS

As Theodore Roosevelt said, "Comparison is the thief of joy." Nobody else is exactly like you, so seek to be the best version of yourself. When you're tempted to compare yourself to someone else, we encourage you to *admire* and be *inspired* by their strengths instead. If you admire certain aspects or qualities about a person, reach out and let them know. This bridge of communication can spark conversation that leads to personal growth in that area.

If you find yourself constantly comparing yourself to others, take note of the kinds of things you're comparing. Is it their income? Their work ethic? Their friends? Their athletic ability? Their job position? Remember, you have the power to change any of these things in your own life if you put your mind to it.

It is so easy to compare your life with the lives of others on social media. If you find that happening frequently, take a social media break. People are only posting the highlights anyway. Rarely do they post their mistakes, missteps, or failures. Filter your feed and rid it of negativity or any posts you feel tempted to compare yourself to.

Focus on becoming the best version of yourself by making the most of your skills, abilities, gifts, personality, and preferences. Don't try to be anyone else.

PREPARE AS MUCH AS POSSIBLE

With any task, in any situation, whether it's a job interview, an assignment you're trying to complete by a certain deadline, a presentation you're going to give, or a meeting with a mentor, if you prepare in advance, you will have much greater success. When you invest time on the front end for any task, you are less likely to be blindsided by a question, problem, or complication that you didn't predict.

Launchers already know this in a university context. If you study for a test, you're going to do better. Even if you already have an extensive understanding of the subject matter, studying beforehand is a good idea. You will be less likely to encounter questions you aren't prepared for.

This same principle applies to every area of your life. Preparation feeds confidence, and confidence helps you do your best in any situation.

BE ACTIVE

A sedentary lifestyle will negatively impact your fitness level, energy, confidence, and overall well-being. The endorphins released when you exercise make you feel better. At the same time, a fitness regimen is all about setting goals and working hard to achieve them, so when you attain those goals, you feel more confident about yourself.

Set fitness goals that are attainable. You're not going to lose a hundred pounds in a week, nor should you try. Maybe you can manage a thirty-minute workout a day, or maybe you can take a nice walk in the morning before you start your day. Take small steps toward self-improvement. With each small goal you achieve, you will feel better about yourself, and that confidence will encourage you to work harder in other areas of your life.

YOU CAN DO THIS

Believe in yourself. That's what confidence is ultimately all about. Since negative self-talk comes so naturally to most of us, intentionally focus on building yourself up. When you're giving a speech, going to an important meeting, or getting ready for a job interview, give yourself a pep talk beforehand. Counteract the negative talk that wants to make you doubt, draw back, or expect the worst.

When you assume you will be good at something, it puts you in the correct state of mind to succeed. That's the essence of confidence. It's believing in your ability to speak in front of an audience. It's your belief that you can do well in an interview. It is your belief in your ability to perform to your strengths. If you believe you will, then you will.

What you say to yourself matters. Develop the habit of constantly encouraging yourself, even when you fail at something. As we told Mary Margaret, "If you keep thinking you belong back in your small hometown, you're going to end up there. If that's your goal in life, that's fine. However, there's a great big world out there, and if you want to go out into that world and carve out a place for yourself, you have to tell yourself you can do it."

DELIVERABLES TO SELF

As you go through your day, make a list of all the negative things you say to yourself. Identify the situations you're in when this happens. At the end of the day, look at your list and imagine how it would affect someone else if you said these things to them.

We have an exercise we like to do with Launchers where we have them bring a photo of themselves when they were children. Then we have them stare at the picture and imagine saying all of those hurtful and discouraging things to that child. Most of the time, they say, "I could never do it. I couldn't be mean to a little kid like that." We've actually had students break down crying during this part of the exercise.

Try this exercise yourself. Maybe, like so many Launchers, you will realize, "I need to stop being so hard on myself. I don't deserve to be talked to this way." Maybe you will become your own best friend rather than your own worst enemy.

THIS JOB DIDN'T WORK OUT, *NOW WHAT?*

The best-laid schemes of mice and men, go often askew.

—ROBERT BURNS, "TO A MOUSE"

A former student of ours who went through graduate school with Codie got a job with a real estate company after graduation. This was shortly after Hurricane Harvey, which hit the Gulf Coast in 2017, and the company did some very unethical things in the aftermath of the storm. They were dishonest in some of their inspections as they attempted to avoid paying for repairs. Ultimately, cutting corners on electrical repairs resulted in a house catching fire.

Although our friend enjoyed the industry and the work, he

didn't want to participate in unethical activity. He knew he had to leave the company and relaunch his career in a different direction.

We helped him adjust his launch criteria, find a new job that matched the new criteria, and he now works in a big office building surrounded by people of integrity. He loves his job, he loves the company culture, and he's much happier.

If you have to relaunch your career, it doesn't mean you failed. We often have to learn some hard lessons before we end up where we truly belong. If you evaluate your first launch correctly, you can relaunch more successfully.

However, in order to relaunch your career, you will have to create your launch criteria. If you haven't done this already, refer back to Chapter Six. You will need your weighted criteria to continue.

QUIT WITH DIGNITY

When you quit a company, make sure you quit with dignity. We've had students get frustrated, suddenly announce, "I'm gone," and walk out on their jobs with no notice and no warning. Sometimes their thinking is, "This job has made me miserable, so I'm going to make them pay." This is never a good idea, no matter how bad of a fit your current position is. Your current company leaders didn't *owe* you a job, and they probably won't miss you when you're gone. You have nothing to gain from trying to penalize them.

If you're thinking about quitting, we strongly encourage you to speak with your mentors and trusted coworkers first. They can help you think through all possible repercussions. For example, if you work for an accounting firm and you quit in March, right in the middle of tax season, you will be forever despised in that industry for leaving your team in the lurch. You can do great harm to your career with this kind of behavior.

Your mentors might also be able to put your frustrations into perspective. "You're having a bad week. Your boss did something that made you mad, but you're in the right place. Hang in there." Since they are removed from the raw emotion of the situation, they can help you step back and consider what's really going on.

With a high degree of emotional intelligence, you will understand the real emotion motivating your desire to quit. This can help you avoid making a rash decision or reacting in an overly emotional way. Instead of allowing negative self-talk to make you act irrationally, consider the source of your disappointment with the job. If your emotions are running high, use some of the self-management techniques from the book *Emotional Intelligence 2.0* by Travis Bradberry and Jean Greaves. Their most basic technique is to "sleep on it" before deciding to quit. Maybe you're just having a bad day. The best job in the world—even the *perfect* job for you—will have bad days, and it would be a tragedy to quit on the spot because of it.

Even if the job was a huge mistake, leaving on the right terms can create references for future jobs. On the other hand, making a big mess on the way out reflects badly on the company and leadership, generating deep resentment that can *only hurt* your future prospects. They trusted you with the position, invested in your hiring and training, and hoped you would be successful. Why burn those bridges just because it wasn't what you wanted?

KEEP YOUR PARACHUTE PACKED

In any job, it's a good idea to keep your parachute packed, but that doesn't mean you should jump out of the airplane. You don't want to find yourself in a situation where you have to leave but can't afford to leave.

We had a student—we'll call him Gavin—who found himself working at a company that clearly wasn't right for him. He was miserable on the job for a variety of reasons, so he finally decided to quit. However, he wasn't ready for a relaunch. Gavin leapt out of the plane with no parachute. As a result, he's been out of work for six months, and he's just wandering around the career world, trying to figure out what to do next.

Job-hoppers get into this kind of trouble all the time. They get frustrated quickly and leave without being prepared for a relaunch. In Chapter One, we mentioned the university dean who told a group of new students, "We know you're going to have four or five jobs by the time you're thirty. That's just what happens." Sadly, this is what students hear in academia and possibly from parents as well.

Don't anticipate having multiple unpleasant jobs before you find something you like. If you do the work of preparation and develop your launch criteria, you can land somewhere great. As a Relauncher, your first job might not have worked out, but that is no indication of a recurring pattern.

Having your parachute ready means you don't leap until you know you can land somewhere safely. It also means you've thought about leaving carefully and planned accordingly before you ever opened the airplane door. To that end, here are some principles to keep in mind before you quit.

GIVE THE JOB ENOUGH TIME

We believe it takes between twelve and eighteen months to evaluate a company and determine if it matches with your career launch criteria—at a bare minimum. If you're thinking about quitting after only five or six months, we strongly encourage you to give it more time. Leaving now is more likely to open you up to job-hopping, and you might just be walking away from long-term prospects for career success.

LEAVE FOR A SPECIFIC REASON

If you're thinking about leaving a job—or if you've been *invited* to leave—think very carefully about *why* it's not working out. Don't quit for vague emotional reasons. We're not suggesting you spend a lot of time indulging the negative self-talk, but if you've stuck it out for eighteen months and the situation is still miserable, take a few minutes of personal quiet time to think about the *specific* reason.

If you're being asked to leave, your company might not be forthcoming about the specific reason for your termination due to legal reasons, so spend some personal quiet time trying to understand why it happened. Be honest with yourself because it will help ensure your relaunch is successful.

We find that many Relaunchers allow the end of a job to

negatively impact their self-confidence. However, if you can correctly identify the reason why the job didn't work out, you will avoid making the same mistake the next time. It can also mitigate the damage to your confidence because you know what went wrong and how to fix it.

DON'T BURN BRIDGES WHEN YOU LEAVE

You might be tempted to give your supervisor a piece of your mind on the way out. While an honest conversation can be useful, emotional retaliation is never a good idea. We've heard of Relaunchers chewing out their bosses, quitting, then patting themselves on the back, thinking, "Well, I guess I told him!" Nothing good will come of this.

You never know how the leaders of the company might benefit you as part of your future network. Maintain these connections by leaving as gracefully as possible. This is especially important if you intend to stay in the same industry.

WHAT'S YOUR PARACHUTE?

Be sure you are prepared for the next job. In the career world, your "parachute" includes an up-to-date résumé, a current portfolio or samples of your work, and an updated contact list for your network. It also means discussing on-the-job problems with your mentors before leaving so you have a healthy perspective on your situation.

Don't make rash decisions. Remember, your career is a marathon, not a sprint. Follow all of the steps and principles we've outlined in this chapter, and you'll have a much softer landing.

STEPS FOR RELAUNCHING YOUR CAREER

When it's time to consider relaunching your career, we recommend the following steps, which will ensure you land successfully.

TAKE A LOOK AT YOUR CAREER LAUNCH CRITERIA

Hopefully, you've kept your career launch criteria from Chapter Six in an easily accessible location. Pull it out and refresh your memory on the criteria you've selected. If you haven't made one, now is the time.

FIX YOUR CRITERIA WEIGHTINGS

It's important to figure out what went wrong. Many Relaunchers fail to do a thorough analysis of their previous job in light of their launch criteria to figure out why it didn't work out. Don't neglect this part of the process, or you run the risk of repeating your mistakes.

Sometimes, Relaunchers think, "My launch criteria didn't help me the first time, so why should I bother?" The fact is, you might not have weighted your criteria accurately the first time. Maybe you gave low weight to the possibility of being away from your partner due to professional travel, only to learn on the job that it made you miserable. If so, you can now go back and give that criterion a much heavier weight on your launch criteria list. Use what you learned about yourself in your first career to fix and improve your launch criteria.

ADD ADDITIONAL CRITERIA

Maybe you forgot some important criteria on your list. Maybe your first career taught you that there are a few things that significantly impact your contentment that you hadn't even considered. Maybe your life changed along the way and some things matter to you now that didn't matter to you then. Whatever the case, if there are any additional criteria that belong on your list, add them now.

MATCH YOUR JOB CRITERIA WITH YOUR LAUNCH CRITERIA

Now that you've adjusted your career launch criteria,

consider your failed job in light of the new list. Would you still have chosen this job over others with the current set of criteria? Maybe you will find that the job still lines up well with your career launch criteria. If so, then it's possible that the job was fine *on paper*, but some other circumstances made it unbearable. This at least tells you that you're in the right industry.

On the other hand, it might become clear to you where you went wrong. You might identify one or more clear misalignments between the job and your *real* career criteria. Maybe you're in the wrong career or industry, and you need to find out where you truly belong.

GET YOUR MENTOR'S INPUT

Now that you've adjusted your career launch criteria, it is imperative that you get feedback from your mentors on the changes. Their knowledge and experience are going to play a huge role in your relaunch. They might be able to help you identify a career, company, or industry that is a better fit than the previous one.

QUIT CORRECTLY

We said it before. We're saying it again. It's that important. If, at this point, it becomes clear that you're in the wrong job, at the wrong company, or in the wrong industry, you need to leave, but do it the right way. Don't throw a tantrum. Don't leave with no notice. Don't burn bridges. Quit with dignity and use your adjusted criteria to find a better career opportunity. You don't have to tell your boss all the reasons why you are quitting, but you do have to tell *yourself*. Just be clear to your boss that you are quitting for a good reason.

DELIVERABLES TO SELF

Now is a good time to go back to your launch criteria list and reconsider your criteria. Make any necessary changes to the criteria on the list or their weightings. It's a living document that needs to be adjusted, so it always provides an accurate reflection of what matters most to you in your career.

We recommend revisiting your launch criteria every six months. At the same time, you can update your résumé and portfolio. Updating this information doesn't mean you're dissatisfied with your current company or career. Do it even if you *love* your job because it keeps you actively evaluating your success and satisfaction. It also prepares you for any possible future.

HUMOR THE BABY BOOMERS (AND HUMOR THE LAUNCHERS)

For many Launchers, the workplace is the first time they find themselves working side by side with people of multiple generations. Though stereotypes can be overblown, there are *distinct differences* between generations that create tension on the job. If you recognize those differences and, more importantly, *understand* the way other generations think and react, it will make it easier to work effectively with people of all ages.

Currently, the primary generational tension in the professional world is between millennials (generally defined as those born between the early 1980s and the year 2000) and baby boomers (those born between 1946 and 1964), so that is what we will deal with primarily in this chapter. However, if you're reading this book a few years down the road, the tension may have shifted to generation Z and generation X. No matter how many years pass, generational distinctions will continue to be a source of tension in the workplace, so it's important to understand each other and learn to communicate effectively.

ASK YOUR MENTOR

Ideally, you have a mentor who is part of a different generation than you. If so, it might be helpful as you're preparing for your career launch to ask them, "What are some of the things young people do that might annoy older leaders?" There might be habits, social practices, or speech patterns that you take for granted which could hinder your career progress. If you know what they are, you can at least moderate what you do and say.

In a sense, by speaking to an older mentor, you are learning about your future boss's potential emotional triggers, many of which you might not even be aware of.

CHECKING YOUR PHONE

There is no starker instance of generational differences than the millennial need to check their phones constantly and the baby boomers' frustration with it. On university campuses, professors struggle with this all the time. Some faculty ban the use of phones in the classroom altogether, but others have simply given up. They know they can't stop the constant texting and checking of social media, so they simply try to ignore it (and continue to feel secretly annoyed about it).

Here's the reality: if you are of a younger generation, checking your phone from time to time probably doesn't seem like a big deal to you. It's a common practice, and it will continue to be a common practice. However, just because you might be used to it doesn't mean it can't do damage to your career. Something you've gotten used to might still be a big deal on the job.

One of our Launchers works for a private equity firm which has ten employees and about fifty investors. Recently, they hired a new marketing manager—a lucrative job that pays about $350,000 a year. During this new employee's very first meeting with investors, while the owner of the company was speaking, he whipped out his phone to check his social media. Right in front of fifteen investors, the owner turned to him and said, "Hey, when we're running these meetings and I'm talking, I want you to pay attention as hard as you possibly can. Don't check your phone."

The marketing manager put his phone away, and the

owner continued to speak. About twenty minutes later, as the meeting continued, the marketing manager pulled out his phone again and began checking social media. The owner pointed to him and said, "That's it. You're fired. Please, leave the building." Security was summoned, the marketing manager was immediately escorted out of the building.

As he walked out of the room, his mouth hung open. He couldn't believe it. The truth is, he probably wasn't trying to antagonize his boss, and he probably didn't intend to be insubordinate. He was used to pulling his phone out from time to time to see if anyone had said anything to him. It was a habit, and he didn't even think about doing it. However, it cost him a $350,000-a-year job.

Baby boomer executives often express their frustration to us about the constant use of cell phones by millennials. They find it incredibly disrespectful, even though younger people usually don't intend it as a sign of disrespect. We've had students tell us they simply *must* check social media at least every fifteen to twenty minutes.

We strongly encourage you to consider how important social media truly is, especially where you career is concerned. If you find yourself constantly checking your phone, even when it hasn't vibrated, buzzed, or lit up, we encourage you to practice *not* checking it. Even having the device sitting on your desk can significantly decrease your productivity.

INTERGENERATIONAL EMOTIONALLY INTELLIGENT DIFFERENCES

When a baby boomer loans something to someone, they expect that person to use it and return it as soon as they are done, but among millennials, it is more common to borrow something and keep it until the owner asks for it back.

Dr. Litzenberg once loaned his parking pass to Codie. The next day, when she hadn't returned it, he confronted her, "Where's my parking pass? Why didn't you bring it back?"

"Sorry, I didn't know you needed it," she replied, handing him the pass. "All you had to do was ask."

"Why did I have to ask?" he replied.

In a broader sense, baby boomers expect things to be put back *exactly where they were* when the borrower is done using them.

We observe this tension all the time. In our seminar room, there are twenty chairs around a big table, and when Launchers use the room for a meeting, they tend to shift the chairs all around the room. When they leave, they typically don't put the chairs back where they were, and it drives the older faculty and staff crazy.

When confronted about it, Launchers will say, "We didn't know you needed them to go back to the same place," but to older staff members that is simply the rule. You put things back where you found them when you're done.

In one of our university departments, there's a classroom with a bunch of tables that have rollers on them so you can easily move them around. Codie had a meeting there once with some Launchers, and she found it very convenient to move the tables around. Later, when the department head came in and saw that the tables had been moved around, he was livid.

"Are these darn kids moving tables around again?" he said. "They should not be moved."

Of course, Codie's thought was, "If they don't need to be moved, why did you buy tables with rollers on them?"

These are simply the *intergenerational emotionally intelligent differences* that we all have to navigate in the professional world, no matter the industry or company. We react differently to emotional triggers, depending on our generation.

At a job fair two years ago, we had a conversation with some young employees representing a company in Utah. We asked, "Why do you like working for this particular company?"

They replied, "Well, for one thing, leaders don't mind if we check Facebook as long as we keep it to once an hour."

"Why do you need to check Facebook once an hour while you're at work?" we asked.

"Well, you never know," they replied. "Someone might have posted something that we need to know about."

This kind of thinking drives most baby boomers crazy. They don't understand it because they were raised in a different context. The need for constant social media connection seems strange. If your future boss is a baby boomer, it's important to realize that something you take for granted, which might not seem like a big deal to you, could be a source of frustration for your boss. It could taint their view of you and have real consequences on your career growth and advancement.

On the other hand, you might find yourself frustrated with your boss if they overreact to something you didn't think was a problem. Dr. Litzenberg had a meeting with a student to discuss a homework assignment, and five minutes into the meeting, the student pulled out her phone and checked a text.

"Is the text important?" Dr. Litzenberg asked. "Is there an emergency?"

The student seemed annoyed by the inquiry. "Yes, it's an emergency," she said, after a moment.

As it turned out, her roommate had texted her to ask what vegetables she wanted for dinner that evening.

UNDERSTANDING EACH OTHER

The purpose of pointing out these differences isn't to condemn any specific generation. This isn't a matter of right and wrong. It's simply about understanding one another so we can navigate an intergenerational work environment.

If you're a millennial or Generation Zer, you simply have to recognize that your baby boomer boss might be sensitive to things that don't bother you. By understanding these differences and avoiding a few key behaviors, you can avoid unnecessary tension on the job.

We've listed three things to help you get started:

- Borrowing things and not returning them

- Moving things around and not putting them back
- Checking your phone (or social media) constantly, especially during meetings

HUMOR THE LAUNCHERS

This next section has two purposes. First, if you are a millennial, it will help you understand yourself and your generation on a deeper level, which is the essence of emotional intelligence.

Second, if you're dealing with intergenerational tensions on the job, you can hand this book to a baby boomer and encourage them to read this section. It might help them deal more effectively with the younger generation entering the workforce.

Millennials hold some very specific values and ideals. These are the most prominent in our experience:

- The idea that anything is possible
- Equal rights
- Extreme loyalty to their children
- The importance of involvement
- Optimism
- Personal gratification
- Questioning everything
- Act now, worry later

- Being team oriented
- Being transformational
- Trusting no one over thirty
- Wanting to make a difference
- Antiwar
- Antigovernment

MAJOR INFLUENCES

Millennials grew up with some distinct influences that have informed the way they approach life. Though they were among the first to grow up at a time when being a child of divorce was generally considered okay, they are also a generation that hopes to fix all the wrong they see in the world.

They were more sheltered than previous generations, with helicopter parents providing a lot of structure for their everyday lives. At the same time, they came of age at a time when America's status as the most prosperous nation seemed threatened. They are one of the first generations to potentially do less well financially than their parents.

CORE VALUES

Millennials love the idea of achievement, and they are avid consumers, which is why so much marketing is directed at them. At the same time, they feel a tremendous sense of civic responsibility, which is why they are more likely to volunteer. When you look at the résumés of millennials, you find that most of them give back to their communities.

They appreciate diversity, both within the workplace and within their friend groups. By utilizing the differences within a group, they are better at coming to consensus than previous generations. They are competitive, but only within areas that interest them, and they want to be purposeful in what they do.

This contributes to a strong desire to know why. Often, when we introduce a new topic to them in one of our learning units, they ask, "Why do we have to learn this? What's the purpose?" Dr. Litzenberg has added a new section to each new learning unit in his classes in which he spends the first few minutes addressing the questions, "Why is this chapter important, and why are we studying it?"

Millennials are the most educated generation in American history, but they are very *now* focused, and they love personal attention, thanks in part to the prevalence of social media and the race for *views* and *likes*. Because of the rapid pace of technological advancement, they are also very big on instant gratification.

WORK ETHIC

Millennials tend to test authority in the workplace, even without realizing they're doing it. They have a general distrust for authority figures. However, they will seek out an authority figure when looking for guidance. Though it might seem like a contradiction, this means they will test their boss frequently, but they will gladly go to their boss for help when they need it.

Boomer bosses sometimes feel like the message from millennials is, "I don't respect you at all, and I'm going to test you constantly, but when I need to make a decision, I'll come to you for advice anyway." In reality, millennials simply want to understand why their boss has set certain rules and made certain priorities. If there's no purpose, then there's no point.

They *really* like the idea of work-life balance. Boomers are hesitant to take a lot of time off work and will often work sixty or seventy hours a week, even if it means being away from family. This is because their generation had a greater fear of losing their jobs. Millennials, on the other hand, want to live a full life outside of work, and they are less willing to work for a company that wants to monopolize their time. We find that there are far fewer workaholics among millennials than boomers.

In general, millennials are looking for a job that is

achievement oriented but strong on collaboration. They love the idea of contributing to a team in a positive, fun, and flexible way, and mentors are very important to them.

They thrive on a team where they feel like they are working with their "buddies," and they expect to work with positive people. If you're a millennial, remember that your baby boomer boss is going to be highly focused on the profitability of the company and might not understand or fully appreciate your need for constant social interaction with your peers.

Millennials also want flexible schedules, and they prefer to be evaluated on their output, not the amount of time they worked. Despite this, they grew up with a lot of structure, so they tend to need it—even if they don't often want it. Without supervision, they often lack discipline, and they don't deal well with difficult people or situations. Many of them have never had to fail, because they were always rewarded as children—the stereotypical "participation trophy" syndrome. To put it another way, they *need* structure, but they *love* autonomy.

COMMUNICATING WITH MILLENNIALS

For boomer bosses to communicate effectively with millennials, they must be positive, respectful, and motivational. If you must criticize, it has to be constructive criticism. Millennials also hate being called out, and they hate seeing others get called out. It feels like bullying, which they are hyperaware of.

Sometimes, in class, we'll show our students a video presentation from a former student so we can give them examples of what to do and what not to do in their own presentations. We'll point out things the former student did well and things they didn't do well.

Often, we will have students approach us afterward and say, "You shouldn't criticize former students like that. They did their best, and you were really rough on them." Bear in mind, we're almost always showing presentations that got an A.

FEEDBACK AND REWARDS

Millennials expect feedback, mostly in the form of encouragement, because they've grown up with it. They received constant feedback from parents. They got praised for every attempt at a soccer goal, got rewarded just for showing up, and received a quick response for everything they did.

This has created both an expectation and a need for both feedback and rewards. A millennial who isn't told they did a good job will quickly feel underappreciated and worry that they are being secretly judged.

ADJUSTING THE APPROACH

A baby boomer boss will more effectively lead millennials if they *shorten the typical feedback cycle*. Boomers came up in a work environment in which annual evaluations were the norm, but as bosses, they might want to consider scheduling monthly meetings in which they offer coaching. It's also more effective to follow the old saying, "Praise in public, correct in private."

When it comes to reinforcing rules, policies, and practices, baby boomers will be more effective if they think about and address the "why." Remember, "We have always done it this way," is viewed negatively by millennials.

UNDERSTANDING EACH OTHER

We do an entire one-day seminar on understanding inter-generational emotional intelligence differences, so it is probably beyond the scope of this section of the book to dive deeply. As we said earlier, the purpose of discussing the distinctions of each generation is not about passing judgment. In fact, it's not a value statement at all. Every generation grows and develops in a unique historical, political, cultural, and economic context, which shapes the way they deal with the world—and respond to emotions—as adults.

The tensions between generations is a reality as old as

humanity itself, but if we can understand each other, we can mitigate some of the tension and work well together. Maybe we can even learn to appreciate one another. When the things your boomer boss does drive you crazy, maybe this chapter will serve as a reminder to take a step back and try to understand where they're coming from so you can contribute to a more collaborative environment. If your boomer boss is having trouble effectively managing millennials, feel free to hand them this book and direct them to this chapter so they can gain a better understanding of where their young workforce is coming from.

19

YOUR PERSONAL BRAND

One of the industry representatives who occasionally speaks to our students has worked for the same company for twenty-eight years. He was asked about the biggest regret of his professional life, and he gave an answer that resonated with us powerfully.

"I let other people build my brand," he said. As he went on to explain, "I relied on my immediate supervisors to tell the people above them about me and share my value to the company. As it turns out, that doesn't happen. You must define your own brand."

IT'S TIME TO THINK BIG

It's time to begin building your own personal *brand*. What do you want other people in the professional world to know about you? That's your brand. Just like Coca-Cola, Pepsi, or Chevrolet, you have to tell the world about yourself, especially if you're thinking *big* for your career, and we hope you *will* think big.

Consider carefully what you want your brand to say about you. If you're interested in management, your brand is going to be very different from someone who wants to go into sales or marketing. Remember, your brand footprint will have a significant reach once it becomes part of your online platforms.

As you've worked through the elements of your career launch, you have already been building the components of your brand. You've identified your strengths, selected your mentors, and thought about what you bring to the table, all of which define aspects of who you are and how you want the professional world to perceive you.

DEFINE YOURSELF

In this chapter, we want to present you with some vital components you can use to define your brand. Not everything we talk about in this chapter will apply to you, but they are here for your consideration.

Your brand is fueled by the information and content you share about yourself. Authenticity is key. If you try to present yourself as something you're not, eventually, you will show your hand, and once people realize you're a phony, your brand will be damaged. However you decide to present yourself to the world, you must communicate with integrity and focus on your *true strengths*. This allows others to learn about your accomplishments and opens up opportunities for collaboration.

When defining your brand, try to think about what makes you unique. Create a distinctive value proposition to differentiate yourself so you will stand out from the others in your industry. When you differentiate yourself, you increase your influence and leverage professional relationships in a positive way. As part of defining your brand, communicate your passions and characteristics in order to align yourself with like-minded people and companies. This will help you find influential advisors.

Along the way, there are key people who have contributed to your personal brand. Recognize their support as part of your brand and thank them. Gratitude is a powerful part of your story.

PERSONAL MISSION STATEMENT

At this point, you may be wondering where to begin. Defining your own brand isn't necessarily something that comes easily to most Launchers. Begin by asking yourself how you want to be seen by the world. What influence do you want to have, particularly in your chosen industry? How do you hope to make an impact? Are you passionate about certain things related to your career aspirations?

Answering these kinds of questions will help you clarify your personal brand. Ultimately, you are communicating what you stand for and what you have to offer. You might not have a lot of experience yet, but even a little bit of experience in college can be transformed into a compelling brand message.

When students are struggling to define their brand, we work with them to develop a personal mission statement. The other day, we were working with a young woman who had a number of job interviews lined up.

"I'm going to do each of these interviews," she said, "and then I'll pick the best one."

"How will you know which one is best?" we asked.

She gave us a confused look. "I guess the one with the best salary and benefits," she replied.

"That's not the best one," we said. "You might end up *hating* the job with the best salary."

We told her to go home that night and create a personal mission statement and bring it back to us the next day. As we explained, a personal mission statement should be a concise statement explaining what you hope to achieve in both your personal and professional life. What impact would you like to make in your industry and possibly in society? What is your larger purpose? What would you like to accomplish in the next twenty or thirty years (in terms of impact, not material possessions)?

We believe everyone has some innate purpose on the earth. Lean into your interests and passions, and your purpose will become clearer to you. Now, simply write it down. Show it to your mentor and others and get feedback. Refine the wording to make it read well, and you've got your personal mission statement. You can continue to tweak and change it over time, but you're ready to start building your brand. All you need is an internet connection.

YOUR ONLINE PRESENCE

Your presence on the internet can make or break you. Google yourself and see what information shows up at the top of the search results. Is it good or bad? Does it present you in the way you want to be presented?

To define your brand, you're going to have to take command of your internet presence. Who are the people searching for you, and how do you want to appear to them? Analyze your social media posts—Facebook, Twitter, Instagram, LinkedIn—and see if there is anything inappropriate, anything you've posted that could damage your brand or reflect poorly on you. Have you posted anything that you wouldn't want to appear at the top of your Google search results?

Social media arguments can be easily accessed, so avoid them. This is easier said than done in the heat of the moment, so always take time to cool down before responding to negativity. Is it even worth responding to? Many of the poisonous exchanges that people get pulled into aren't even worth the mental energy. Every negative comment on a social media post doesn't need or deserve a response. It might be better to let it go. As author and speaker Rachel Hollis says, "Someone else's opinion of you is none of your business."[10] Let them go negative while you continue living your best life.

PERSONAL WEBSITE

A personal website gives you the chance to select a catchy name for yourself or your business. Though millions

---

10   Rachel Hollis, Facebook, December 21, 2017, https://www.facebook.com/99908631258/ posts/someone-elses-opinion-of-you-is-none-of-your-business-youre-afraid-to-move-forwa/10155794238401259/.

of catchy names have already been claimed, there are still plenty of options. For examples of what a personal website might look like, check out kerrylitzenberg.com, codiewright.com, and golaunchyourcareer.com.

Create a short video for your website that demonstrates your speaking ability and introduces you to anyone who lands on your page. If you've written any papers on relevant topics, link to them.

Developing a nice-looking, mobile-friendly, and user-friendly website isn't easy. If it's not your forte, consider hiring someone else to do it. A poorly designed website will reflect badly on you. Select keywords that resonate with what you're trying to say about yourself, and use these words throughout your website to increase search engine optimization.

You want a website that looks professional and stylish, is easy to navigate, and has a logo and color palette that resonates with you. Promote the website on your social media profiles.

LINKEDIN

LinkedIn is one of the most useful platforms for spreading your brand. Carefully craft your LinkedIn profile to showcase the most important skills for your career goals and connect with like-minded people who are experts in your industry. Don't approach this social media platform the way you would Facebook or Instagram. You don't want to add your kindergarten teacher or people you knew in junior high. Vet your connections in a way that establishes you professionally.

Always behave with the utmost professionalism on LinkedIn. Avoid acting—or reacting—emotionally, posting irrelevant photos (no one needs to see a cute picture of your cat attacking a string), or anything that might be off-putting to people in your industry. Generally speaking, it's best to avoid political topics on LinkedIn, unless politics is your industry, because it will generate negativity that can damage your brand.

PERSONAL BLOG

A personal blog is a place to show the world your expertise, professional passions, industry knowledge, and personality. Don't blog about your trip to the grocery store. Your goal is to present a regular stream of posts on relevant topics. Don't just post one time and forget about the blog, and don't hop from topic to topic. If you're talking about something specific, stick with it for a few weeks to generate interest.

Avoid topics that are controversial to your target audience.

Be careful with religion or morally based issues, unless they are specifically relevant to your industry. Of course, this varies from industry to industry. If you're in politics, a political post isn't necessarily shocking to anyone. However, if you're in sales, a political post can be detrimental to your business. People respond to controversy with emotion rather than facts, and a negative response can get attached to your brand image.

It's fair to mention your personal beliefs, but be respectful of others. People love to hear personal stories from your life, as long as they're relevant to your target audience. However, there's a fine line between authenticity and vulnerability. Remember, your traffic will be mostly comprised of people with similar interests, so aim to educate, inspire, and motivate them. Invite your audience to join the conversation, but be prepared for occasional brutal honesty. Don't overreact when responding to such feedback. Not everyone's going to like your content, and you need to be okay with that if you're going to put your stuff online. Listen to your community of followers, if you have one, to find out what they want to hear.

YOUTUBE VIDEOS

A YouTube channel can be an effective part of your personal brand as long as the videos you post generate interest with the right people. Dozens of videos of your latest family vacation probably won't contribute to your career unless you're in the travel industry. As with your blog, you want to present videos that showcase your skills and relevant experiences. If you participate in an industry-related competition in college, showcase it on your channel.

We all know that YouTube is overflowing with videos of millennials chugging gallons of root beer or reviewing fast-food cheeseburgers. While there's an audience for these kinds of videos, they probably won't build your brand.

Ideally, your videos showcase the professional you. Put on your best suit or dress and talk about your career dreams, desires, interests, and experiences. These are the kinds of videos that will appeal to company leaders.

SPEAKING ENGAGEMENTS

For most people, speaking in front of a crowd is terrifying. Your heart is pounding, your hands are sweating, and your stomach is in knots. We've all been there. On the other hand, you might be one of those rare few who yearns to be on stage at conferences. If that's the case, we encourage you to join a local Toastmasters club and develop your speaking ability. They can also help you get over the fear of speaking.

Being able to stand up in front of a crowd and command their attention is an ability not to be taken lightly. If you can captivate an audience, you could become a popular subject matter expert, which will open numerous doors of opportunity in your career.

It's not hard to develop a TED Talk if you have something to say and you're willing to say it. Connect with the people who organize local TED Talks and refine your message. When you begin speaking, video and review your performance. This can feel weird at first, but it's the best way to improve.

KEEP BUILDING YOUR BRAND

You don't build your brand overnight. You lay a foundation, and then you create it a brick at a time. Highly influential entrepreneurs and professionals like Warren Buffet have worked on their brand for decades, continuing to reinforce it with every speech they give, article they write, and choice they make.

Protect your brand. It doesn't take much to undo years of positivity. Continue to pursue that higher purpose in your life so your words don't ring hollow. When you commit to making an impact, you will go farther than you ever thought possible.

CONCLUSION

In this book, we've looked at four distinct aspects of your career launch. In Part One, we discussed the importance of developing the right mindset, identifying your career launch criteria, and putting together your career launch plan.

In Part Two, we helped you figure out what you bring to the table, which skills, gifts, abilities, and experience you have to offer, and then we talked about building your résumé in a way that differentiates you.

In Part Three, we delved into the seven core competencies that you need to develop in order to thrive in a career environment: *mentoring, interviewing, networking, job shadowing, professionalism, travel*, and *reading*.

Finally, in Part Four, we looked beyond your career launch to discuss some of the challenges related to thriving on the job, from overcoming negative self-talk to dealing with intergenerational conflict. We also talked about what to do if a job doesn't work out, and we showed you the importance of building your personal brand.

With most books, when you finish reading it, you're done. You put it back on the shelf, loan it to someone else, return it to the library, take it to the half-price used book sale, or leave it on the seat of the airplane as you disembark. Some of the insights might linger with you (especially if you follow our advice from Chapter Fifteen and take notes), but you don't need to keep the book within easy reach.

However, when we wrote this book, we didn't intend for you to absorb everything on the first pass. Ideally, your career launch won't unfold fast enough to implement the recommendations in every chapter during your first reading. Instead, your first pass is intended to give you an overview of the road ahead.

Keep the book on your nightstand or on your desk—somewhere within easy reach—so you can refer back to the chapters most relevant to where are you are in your career launch. For example, when it's time to write or polish your résumé, you can pull the book down and reference that chapter. You might also read a little bit from time to time just to reinforce your understanding of the journey.

Even after you start your career, you can refer back to some of this content. For example, a question might arise about professionalism in the workplace. Turn to the chapter of professionalism and refresh your memory. If you're dealing with intergenerational conflict on the job, turn back to that chapter because it will be more relevant than when you first read the book.

We look forward to the great things you're going to achieve in your career. You have everything you need, so start putting your career launch plans into action.

Good luck and Godspeed.

Now, go launch your career.

ABOUT THE AUTHORS

DR. KERRY LITZENBERG is Presidential Professor for Teaching Excellence and Regents Professor at Texas A&M University. After forty years of teaching at Texas A&M, he has had more than thirteen thousand students in his classroom. In addition, Dr. Litzenberg has counseled hundreds of students about their career launches, helping them identify their skills and the launch criteria they should use to evaluate job opportunities. He earned a PhD in Agricultural Economics, a master's degree in counseling, and a bachelor of science degree in education. Dr. Litzenberg has worked in Australia, Indonesia, France, Italy, Canada, and at more than a dozen universities across the United States.

CODIE WRIGHT is the assistant director of the Weston AgriFood Sales Program at Texas A&M University. She earned a bachelor's degree in leadership and development and received a master's in agribusiness from Texas A&M University. Over the past five years, Codie has worked closely with Dr. Litzenberg to counsel students about their career launches. Codie is a certified Gallup's Strengths Assessment Instructor and a Giant 5 Voices Consultant. She collaborates with industry representatives and students to bridge the gap between industry and academia. Her mission to serve others, mentor students, and encourage people to launch their careers is visible in both the classroom and through speaking engagements.

Dr. Litzenberg and Codie have formed a unique and powerful partnership they call a *boomerillennium*, combining the experiences and perspectives of a baby boomer and a millennial, which allows them to speak to the unique challenges of entering the workforce today.

ACKNOWLEDGMENTS

This book would not have become a reality without the professional, personal, and financial support of Graham Weston. His admonition that we needed to get these guidelines down in a book that could cause transformational change ultimately led to this book's creation.

After selling Rackspace, the internet storage company he created, for over $3 billion, Graham devoted himself to changing downtown San Antonio into an information center for young people. Graham has created the coworking space Geekdom as a business incubator for tech firms and purchased several properties in downtown San Antonio to attract young technical specialists. He was recently selected as a distinguished alumnus of Texas A&M University, the highest honor the university awards, and he retrofitted real estate property for emergency housing in the aftermath of hurricanes. That's as close to a ninja billionaire as we've ever seen.

For your motivation, foresight, and encouragement, we thank you, Graham Weston.

We also want to thank the thousands of students at Texas A&M who have provided the stories in this book. You are all truly the inspiration behind our commitment to the educational process. We particularly want to thank those students and teaching assistants who have helped *us* to learn about launching a career.

We're grateful for Jeffrey Miller, our Scribe, who helped us with the manuscript. We could not have developed this first book without you.

Finally, we want to thank all of the industry representatives who have worked alongside us these past years by sharing their career development wisdom with our students and with us. You are a valued part of our career launch team.

Made in the USA
Las Vegas, NV
29 September 2021

Made in the USA
Lexington, KY
10 December 2014